THE VISUAL DICTIONARY *of*
FLIGHT

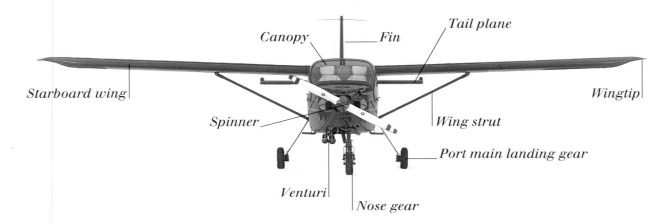

Canopy Fin Tail plane

Starboard wing Wingtip

Spinner Wing strut

Port main landing gear

Venturi

Nose gear

ARV SUPER 2 MODERN LIGHT AIRCRAFT

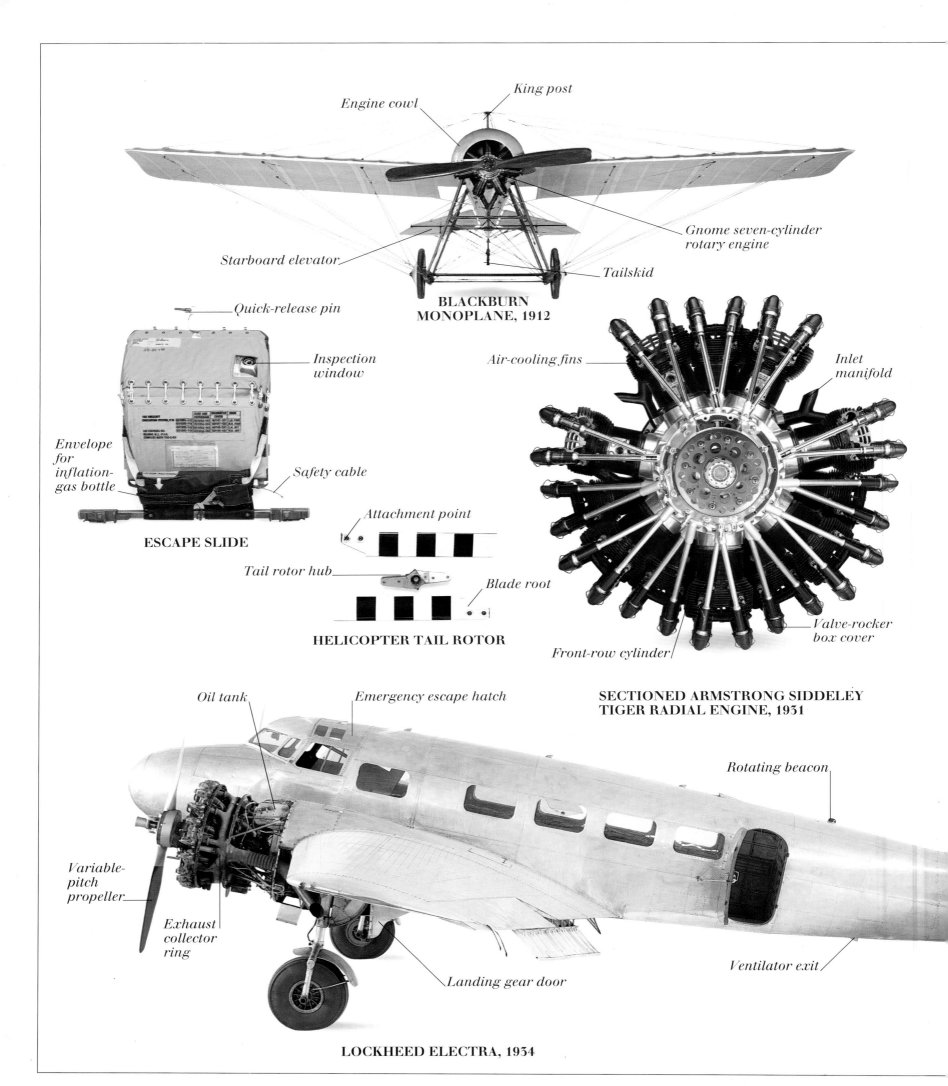

Engine cowl

King post

Starboard elevator

Gnome seven-cylinder
rotary engine

Tailskid

**BLACKBURN
MONOPLANE, 1912**

Quick-release pin

Inspection
window

Air-cooling fins

Inlet
manifold

Envelope
for
inflation-
gas bottle

Safety cable

ESCAPE SLIDE

Attachment point

Tail rotor hub

Blade root

HELICOPTER TAIL ROTOR

Valve-rocker
box cover

Front-row cylinder

**SECTIONED ARMSTRONG SIDDELEY
TIGER RADIAL ENGINE, 1931**

Oil tank

Emergency escape hatch

Rotating beacon

Variable-
pitch
propeller

Exhaust
collector
ring

Landing gear door

Ventilator exit

LOCKHEED ELECTRA, 1934

EYEWITNESS VISUAL DICTIONARIES

THE VISUAL DICTIONARY *of*

FLIGHT

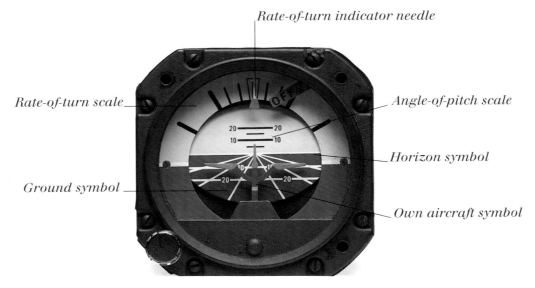

Rate-of-turn indicator needle

Rate-of-turn scale

Angle-of-pitch scale

Horizon symbol

Ground symbol

Own aircraft symbol

ARTIFICIAL HORIZON FLIGHT INSTRUMENT

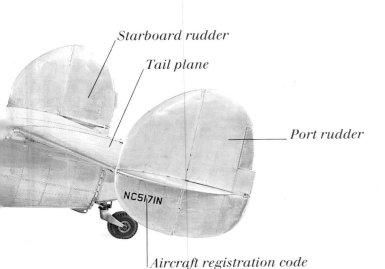

Starboard rudder

Tail plane

Port rudder

NC517N

Aircraft registration code

A DK PUBLISHING BOOK

PROJECT ART EDITOR ANDREW NASH
DESIGNER LESLEY BETTS

PROJECT EDITOR PAUL DOCHERTY
EDITOR FIONA COURTENAY-THOMPSON
CONSULTANT EDITOR BILL GUNSTON
U.S. CONSULTANT NIGEL MOLL
U.S. EDITOR CHARLES A. WILLS

MANAGING ART EDITOR STEPHEN KNOWLDEN
SENIOR EDITOR MARTYN PAGE
MANAGING EDITOR RUTH MIDGLEY

PHOTOGRAPHY PETER ANDERSON, MARTIN CAMERON, STEVE GORTON, JAMES STEVENSON
ILLUSTRATIONS MICK GILLAH, DAVE PUGH, CHRIS WOOLMER

PRODUCTION HILARY STEPHENS

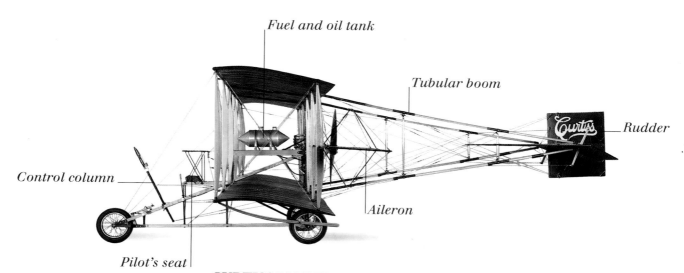

Fuel and oil tank

Tubular boom

Rudder

Control column

Aileron

Pilot's seat

CURTISS MODEL-D PUSHER, 1911

FIRST AMERICAN EDITION, 1992

10 9 8 7 6 5 4 3

DK PUBLISHING, INC.,
95 MADISON AVENUE,
NEW YORK, NEW YORK, 10016

COPYRIGHT © 1992 DORLING KINDERSLEY LIMITED, LONDON

VISIT US ON THE WORLD WIDE WEB AT
HTTP://WWW.DK.COM

LIBRARY OF CONGRESS CATALOGING-IN-PUBLICATION DATA

THE EYEWITNESS VISUAL DICTIONARY OF FLIGHT. — 1ST AMERICAN ED.
p. cm. — (THE EYEWITNESS VISUAL DICTIONARIES)
INCLUDES INDEX.
SUMMARY: TEXT AND LABELED ILLUSTRATIONS DEPICT A VARIETY OF HISTORIC AND MODERN AIRCRAFT
AND THEIR COMPONENTS, AS WELL AS AVIATION-RELATED EQUIPMENT.

ISBN 1–56458–101–2
1. AIRPLANES—TERMINOLOGY—JUVENILE LITERATURE.
2. AIRPLANES—PICTORIAL WORKS—JUVENILE LITERATURE.
3. AERONAUTICS—TERMINOLOGY—JUVENILE LITERATURE.
4. AERONAUTICS—PICTORIAL WORKS—JUVENILE LITERATURE.
5. PICTURE DICTIONARIES, ENGLISH—JUVENILE LITERATURE.
[1. AIRPLANES. 2. AERONAUTICS.] I. SERIES.
TL547.E85 1992
629. 133'014—dc20   92–7670
                                                            CIP
                                                            AC

REPRODUCED BY COLOURSCAN, SINGAPORE
PRINTED AND BOUND IN ITALY BY ARNOLDO MONDADORI, VERONA

120° cowl panel

Spinner

Contents

120° cowl segment

**ENGINE COWLS OF A
LOCKHEED ELECTRA, 1934**

Parabolic reflector

*Radar receiver
and transmitter*

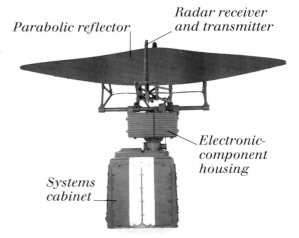

*Electronic-
component
housing*

*Systems
cabinet*

AIRFIELD RADAR, 1953

Backplate

Spinner

Flanged plate

**PROPELLER OF A MODERN LIGHT
AIRCRAFT**

Parachute riser

*Personal
survival pack*

Rocket pack

**MODERN EJECTOR
SEAT**

Horseshoe magnet

Distributor

*Helical
drive gear*

MAGNETO, 1911

Steering stop

Damper unit

Hoop

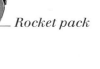

Axle bolt

**NOSE GEAR OF A MODERN
LIGHT AIRCRAFT**

Balloons and airships

THE FIRST SUSTAINED FLIGHT was made by the French Montgolfier brothers' hot-air balloon in 1783. Their balloon was made of paper, and the hot air (which provided the lift) was produced by burning straw. Later balloons were filled with various lighter-than-air gases (hydrogen, helium, or coal gas) until about 1970, when hot-air balloons again became fashionable. In modern hot-air balloons, the air is heated by propane burners carried in the balloon's basket. Modern airships may be filled with helium or hot air (hydrogen, used in early airships, is dangerously inflammable). Unlike balloons, airships have some means of propulsion and can be steered. Many modern airships also have swiveling propellers to assist with takeoff and landing. The first airship was made in Paris, France, in 1852, but the best-known airship maker was the German Count Ferdinand von Zeppelin, who built his first craft in 1900. Airships made the first intercontinental passenger flights and were a popular form of transport until the 1930s, when the disastrous crashes of the British *R101* and the German *Hindenburg* led to a virtual halt in airship production. Small airships were used as convoy escorts in both world wars, and today they are used for surveillance and for aerial advertising.

Varnished, painted envelope of handmade paper

Painted emblem

Strengthened, glued paper ring

Supporting cord

Pitchfork for fueling fire

Opening to fire

Gallery for passengers and straw

Dip tube (feeds liquid valve)

Float

SECTIONED GAS CYLINDER

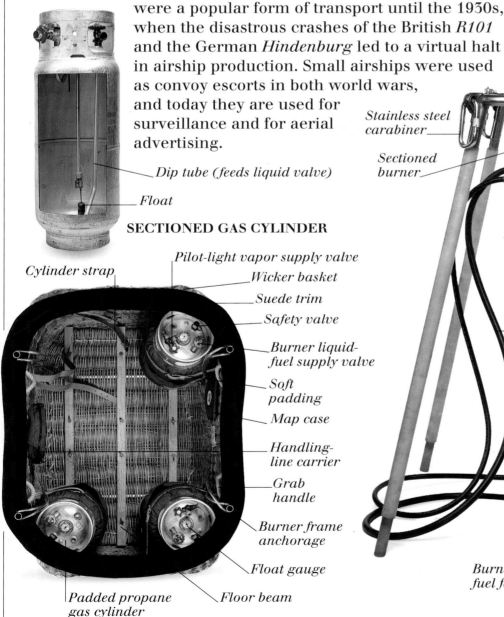

Cylinder strap

Pilot-light vapor supply valve

Wicker basket

Suede trim

Safety valve

Burner liquid-fuel supply valve

Soft padding

Map case

Handling-line carrier

Grab handle

Burner frame anchorage

Float gauge

Padded propane gas cylinder

Floor beam

HOT-AIR BALLOON BASKET

Hot coil to vaporize fuel

Stainless steel burner frame

Pilot-light valve lever

Main blast-valve lever

Stainless steel carabiner

Sectioned burner

Pilot light

Jet ring

Crossover valve

Handle

Liquid-fire valve (cowburner)

Burner liquid-fuel feed pipe

Nylon strut

Padded protective cover

Pilot-light fuel-vapor feed pipe

Burner liquid-fuel feed connector

Pilot-light fuel-vapor feed pipe

Basket support cable

SECTIONED HOT-AIR BALLOON BURNER

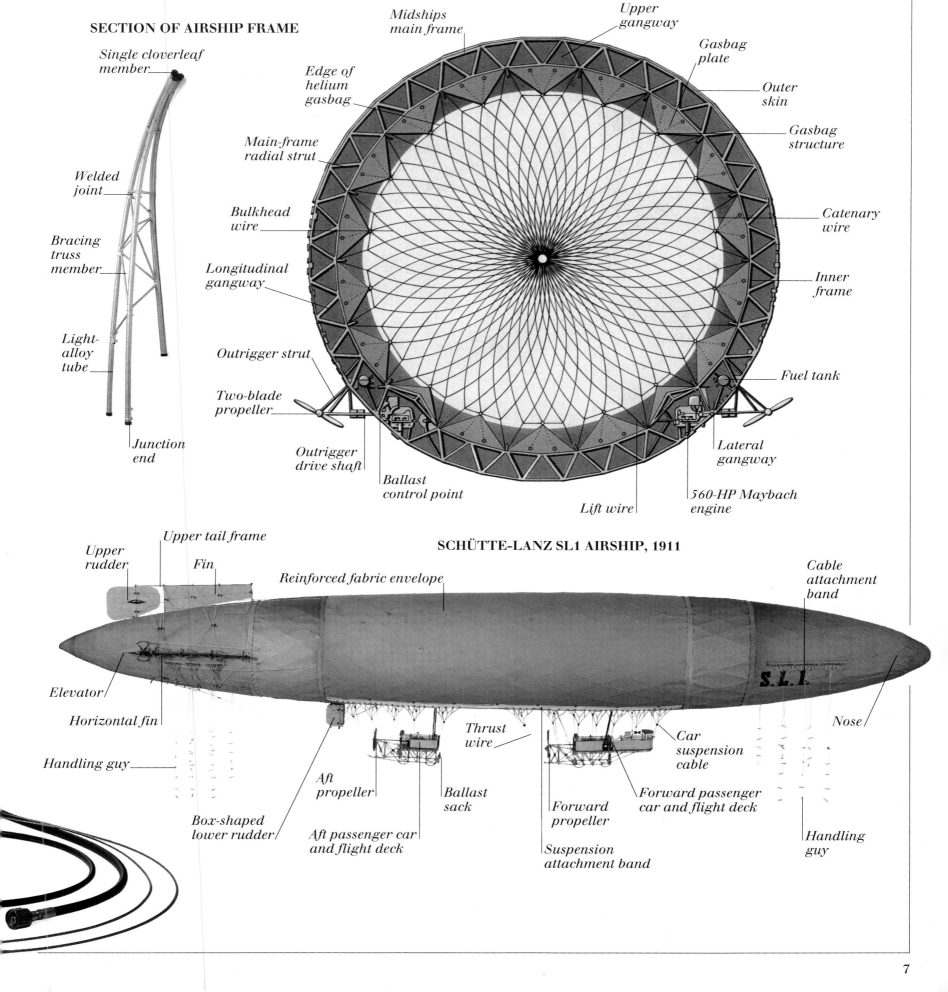

CROSS-SECTION OF USS AKRON AIRSHIP, 1931

SECTION OF AIRSHIP FRAME

Single cloverleaf member

Welded joint

Bracing truss member

Light-alloy tube

Junction end

Midships main frame

Edge of helium gasbag

Main-frame radial strut

Bulkhead wire

Longitudinal gangway

Outrigger strut

Two-blade propeller

Outrigger drive shaft

Ballast control point

Upper gangway

Gasbag plate

Outer skin

Gasbag structure

Catenary wire

Inner frame

Fuel tank

Lateral gangway

Lift wire

560-HP Maybach engine

SCHÜTTE-LANZ SL1 AIRSHIP, 1911

Upper tail frame

Upper rudder

Fin

Reinforced fabric envelope

Cable attachment band

Elevator

Horizontal fin

Handling guy

Aft propeller

Box-shaped lower rudder

Aft passenger car and flight deck

Thrust wire

Ballast sack

Forward propeller

Suspension attachment band

Car suspension cable

Forward passenger car and flight deck

Nose

S.L.I.

Handling guy

Pioneers of flight

FLIGHT HAS FASCINATED MANKIND for centuries, and countless unsuccessful flying machines have been designed. The first successful flight was made by the French Montgolfier brothers in 1783, when they flew a balloon over Paris (see pp. 6-7). The next major advance was the development of gliders, notably by the Englishman Sir George Cayley, who in 1845 designed the first glider to make a sustained flight, and by the German Otto Lilienthal, who became known as the world's first pilot because he managed to achieve controlled flights. However, powered flight did not become a practical possibility until the invention of lightweight, gas-driven internal-combustion engines at the end of the 19th century. Then, in 1903, the American brothers Orville and Wilbur Wright made the first powered flight in their Wright Flyer biplane, which used a four-cylinder, gas-driven engine. Aircraft design advanced rapidly, and in 1909 the Frenchman Louis Blériot made his pioneering flight across the English Channel (see pp. 10-11). The American Glenn Curtiss also achieved several "firsts" in his Model-D Pusher and its variants, most notably winning the world's first competition for airspeed at Reims in 1909.

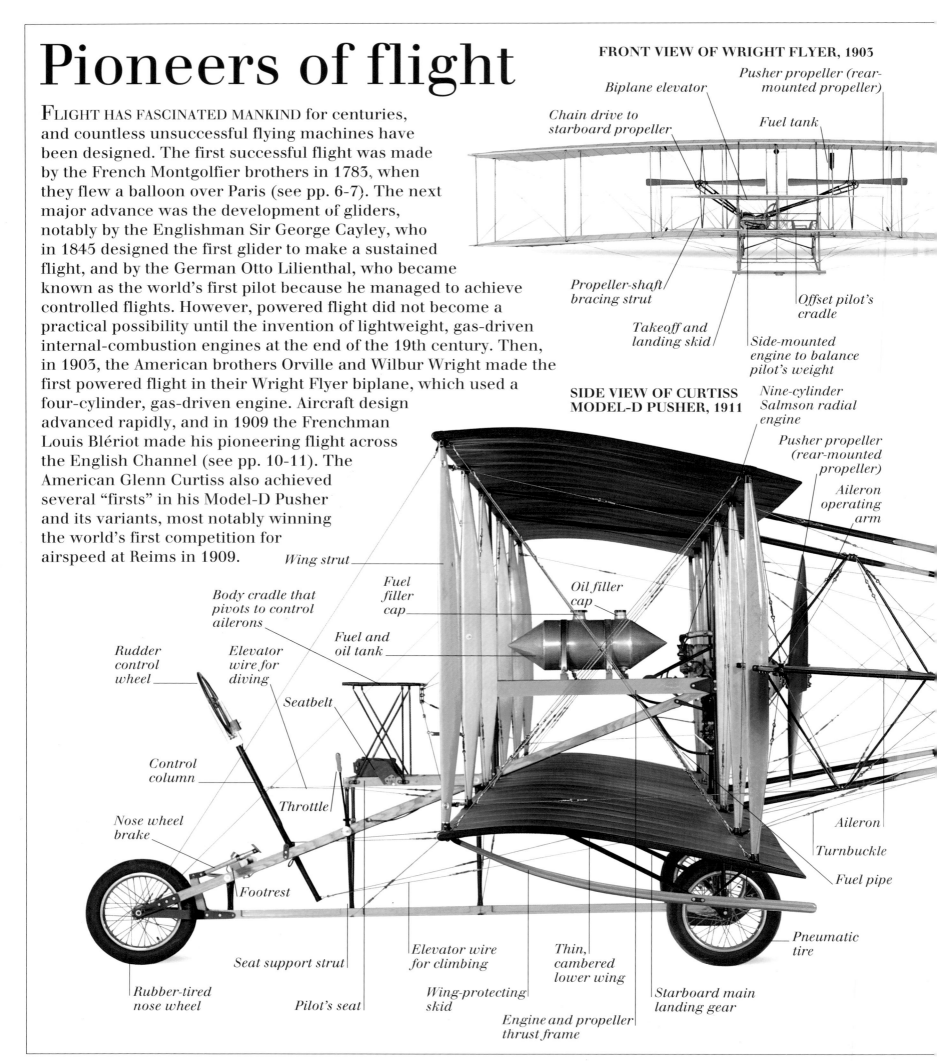

FRONT VIEW OF WRIGHT FLYER, 1903

Biplane elevator

Pusher propeller (rear-mounted propeller)

Chain drive to starboard propeller

Fuel tank

Propeller-shaft bracing strut

Takeoff and landing skid

Offset pilot's cradle

Side-mounted engine to balance pilot's weight

SIDE VIEW OF CURTISS MODEL-D PUSHER, 1911

Nine-cylinder Salmson radial engine

Pusher propeller (rear-mounted propeller)

Aileron operating arm

Wing strut

Body cradle that pivots to control ailerons

Fuel filler cap

Oil filler cap

Fuel and oil tank

Rudder control wheel

Elevator wire for diving

Seatbelt

Control column

Throttle

Nose wheel brake

Footrest

Aileron

Turnbuckle

Fuel pipe

Pneumatic tire

Rubber-tired nose wheel

Seat support strut

Pilot's seat

Elevator wire for climbing

Wing-protecting skid

Thin, cambered lower wing

Starboard main landing gear

Engine and propeller thrust frame

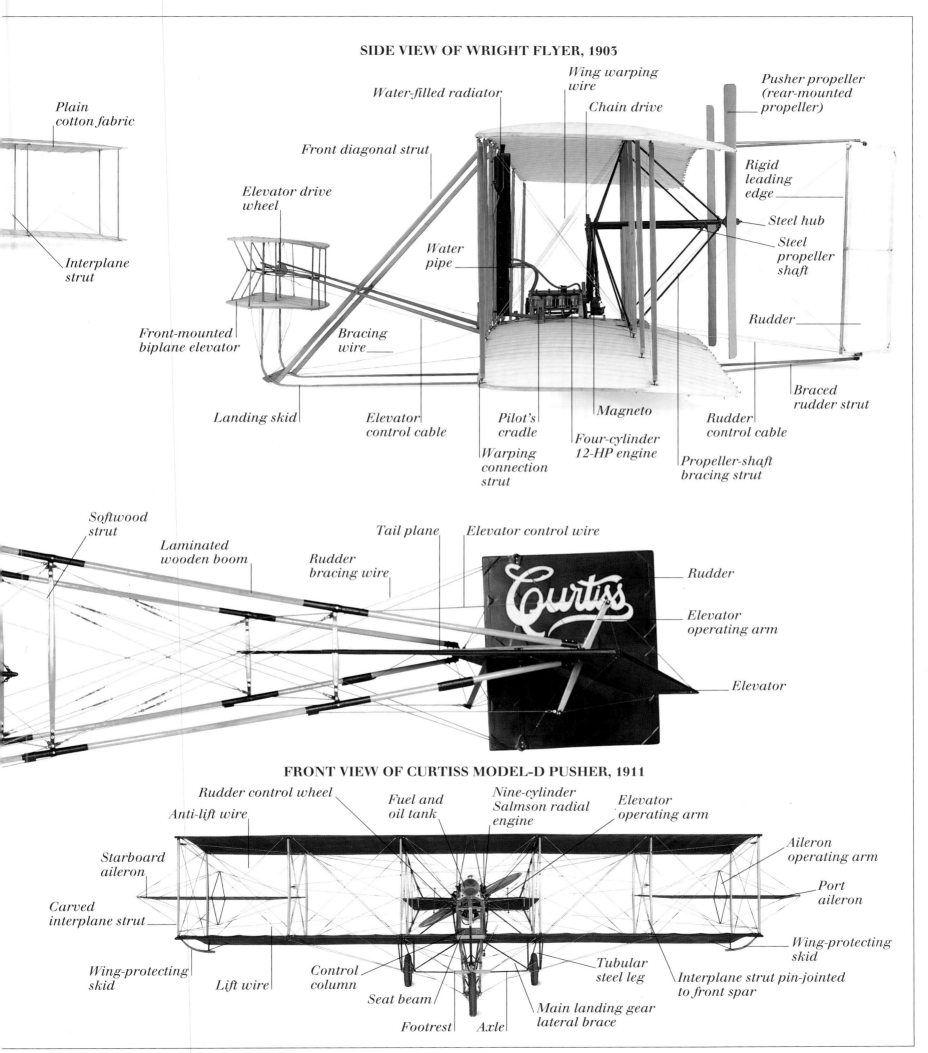

SIDE VIEW OF WRIGHT FLYER, 1903

Plain cotton fabric

Interplane strut

Wing warping wire

Water-filled radiator

Chain drive

Pusher propeller (rear-mounted propeller)

Front diagonal strut

Elevator drive wheel

Rigid leading edge

Steel hub

Steel propeller shaft

Water pipe

Front-mounted biplane elevator

Bracing wire

Rudder

Landing skid

Elevator control cable

Pilot's cradle

Magneto

Rudder control cable

Braced rudder strut

Warping connection strut

Four-cylinder 12-HP engine

Propeller-shaft bracing strut

Softwood strut

Laminated wooden boom

Tail plane

Elevator control wire

Rudder

Rudder bracing wire

Elevator operating arm

Elevator

FRONT VIEW OF CURTISS MODEL-D PUSHER, 1911

Rudder control wheel

Fuel and oil tank

Nine-cylinder Salmson radial engine

Elevator operating arm

Anti-lift wire

Aileron operating arm

Starboard aileron

Port aileron

Carved interplane strut

Wing-protecting skid

Wing-protecting skid

Lift wire

Control column

Seat beam

Tubular steel leg

Interplane strut pin-jointed to front spar

Footrest

Axle

Main landing gear lateral brace

Early monoplanes

RUMPLER MONOPLANE, 1908

MONOPLANES HAVE ONE WING on each side of the fuselage. The principal disadvantage of this arrangement in early wooden-framed aircraft was that single wings were weak. They required strong wires to brace them to king posts above and below the fuselage. However, single wings also had advantages: they experienced less drag than multiple wings, allowing greater speed; they also made aircraft more maneuverable because single wings were easier to warp (twist) than double wings, and warping the wings was how pilots controlled the roll of early aircraft. By 1912, the French pilot Louis Blériot had used a monoplane to make the first flight across the English Channel, and the Briton Robert Blackburn and the Frenchman Armand Deperdussin had proved the greater speed of monoplanes. However, a spate of crashes caused by broken wings discouraged monoplane production, except in Germany, where all-metal monoplanes were developed in 1917. The wings of all-metal monoplanes did not need strengthening by struts or bracing wires, but despite this, such planes were not widely adopted until the 1930s.

FRONT VIEW OF BLACKBURN MONOPLANE, 1912

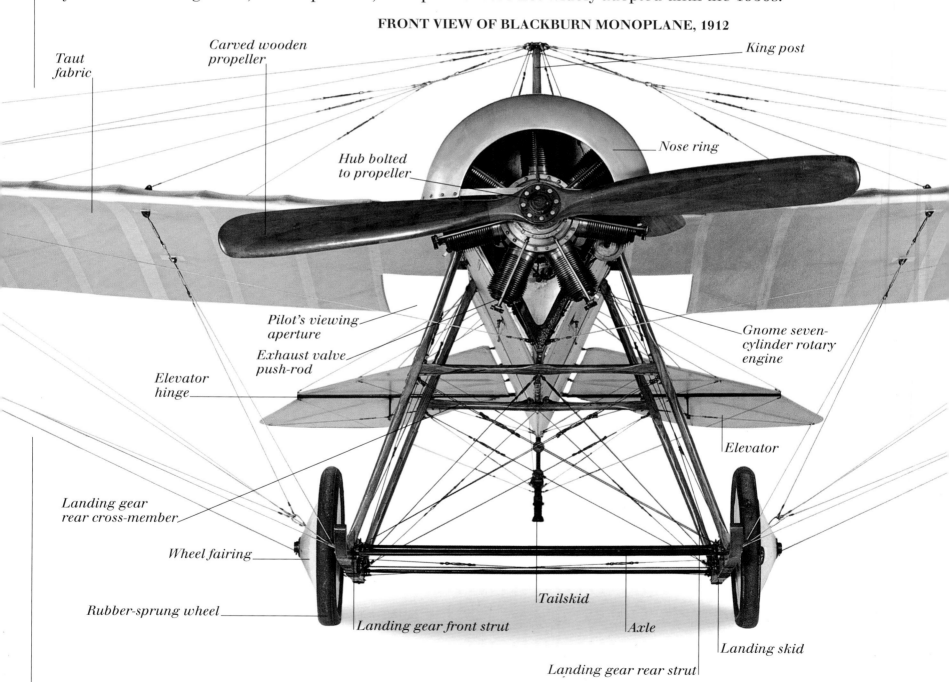

Taut fabric

Carved wooden propeller

King post

Nose ring

Hub bolted to propeller

Pilot's viewing aperture

Gnome seven-cylinder rotary engine

Exhaust valve push-rod

Elevator hinge

Elevator

Landing gear rear cross-member

Wheel fairing

Rubber-sprung wheel

Landing gear front strut

Tailskid

Axle

Landing skid

Landing gear rear strut

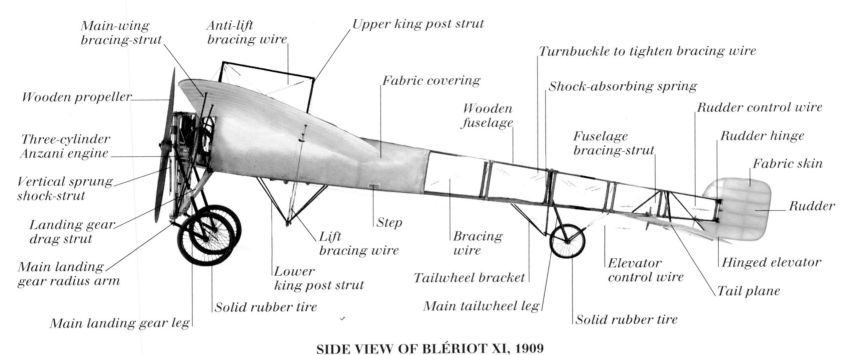

Main-wing bracing-strut

Anti-lift bracing wire

Upper king post strut

Turnbuckle to tighten bracing wire

Wooden propeller

Fabric covering

Shock-absorbing spring

Three-cylinder Anzani engine

Wooden fuselage

Rudder control wire

Rudder hinge

Fabric skin

Vertical sprung shock-strut

Fuselage bracing-strut

Rudder

Landing gear drag strut

Main landing gear radius arm

Lift bracing wire

Step

Bracing wire

Elevator control wire

Hinged elevator

Main landing gear leg

Lower king post strut

Tailwheel bracket

Main tailwheel leg

Solid rubber tire

Tail plane

Solid rubber tire

SIDE VIEW OF BLÉRIOT XI, 1909

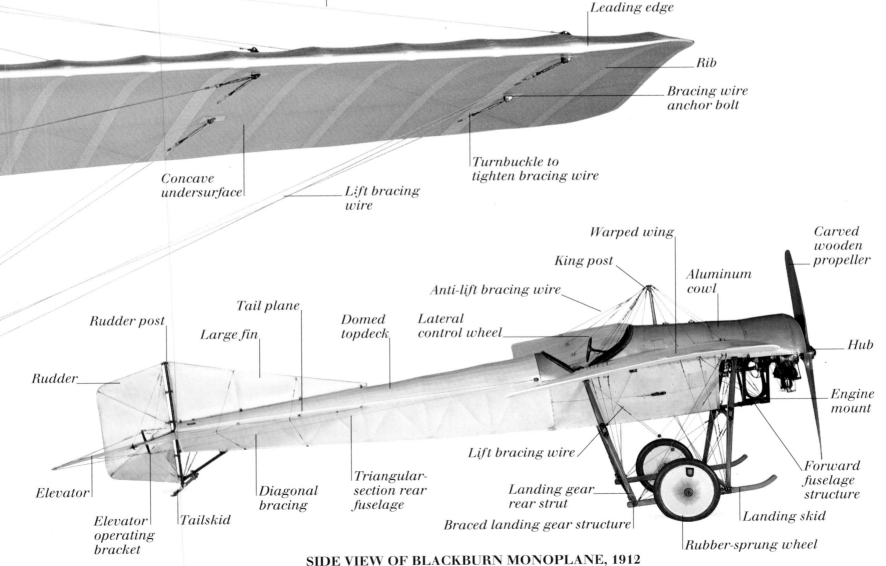

Anti-lift bracing wire

Leading edge

Rib

Bracing wire anchor bolt

Concave undersurface

Turnbuckle to tighten bracing wire

Lift bracing wire

Warped wing

King post

Carved wooden propeller

Anti-lift bracing wire

Aluminum cowl

Rudder post

Tail plane

Domed topdeck

Lateral control wheel

Large fin

Hub

Rudder

Engine mount

Lift bracing wire

Elevator

Diagonal bracing

Triangular-section rear fuselage

Landing gear rear strut

Forward fuselage structure

Elevator operating bracket

Tailskid

Braced landing gear structure

Landing skid

Rubber-sprung wheel

SIDE VIEW OF BLACKBURN MONOPLANE, 1912

Biplanes and triplanes

BIPLANES DOMINATED AIRCRAFT DESIGN until the 1930s, largely because some early monoplanes (see pp. 10-11) were too fragile to withstand the stresses of flight. The struts between biplanes' wings made the wings strong compared with those of early monoplanes, although the greater surface area of biplanes' wings increased drag and reduced speed. Many aircraft designers also developed triplanes, which had a particular advantage over biplanes: more wings meant a shorter wingspan to achieve the same lifting power, and a shorter wingspan gave greater maneuverability. Triplanes were most successful as fighters during World War I, the German Fokker triplane being a notable example. However, the greater maneuverability of triplanes was no advantage for normal flying, and so most manufacturers continued to make biplanes. Many other aircraft designs were attempted. Some were quadruplanes, with four pairs of wings. Some had tandem wings (two pairs of monoplane wings, one behind the other). One of the most bizarre designs was by the Englishman Horatio Phillips; it had 20 sets of narrow wings and looked rather like a Venetian blind.

LAMINATED PROPELLER

SIDE VIEW OF AVRO TRIPLANE IV, 1910

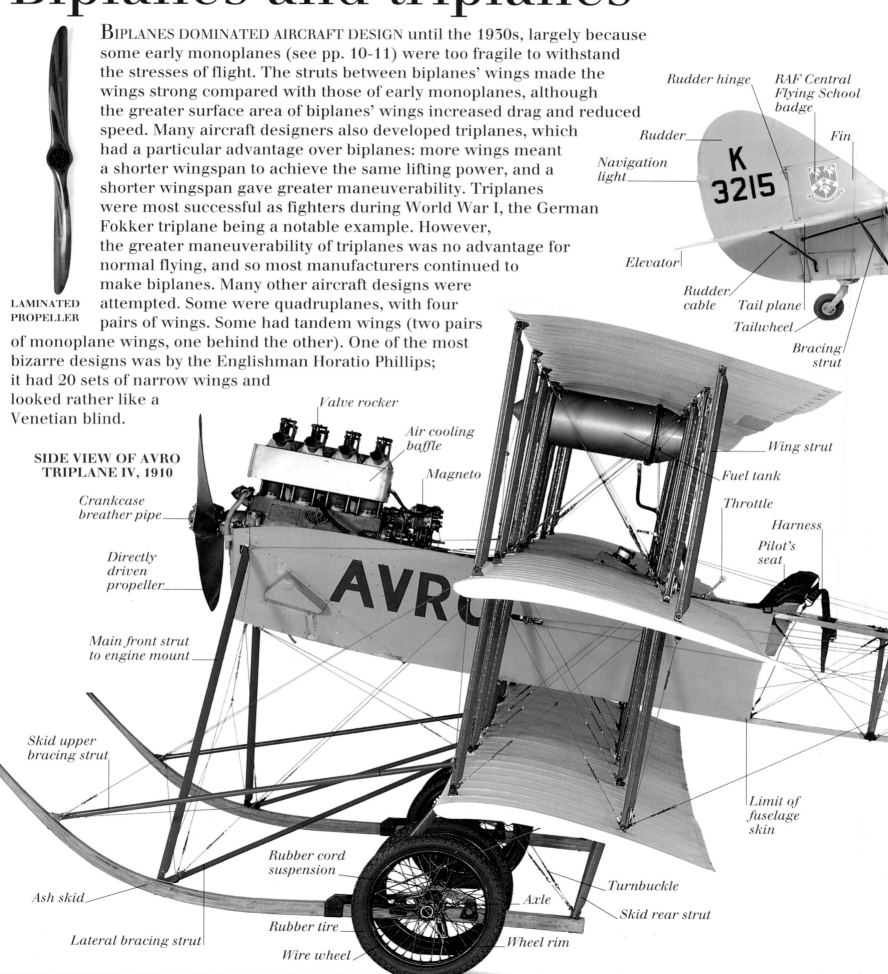

Rudder hinge

RAF Central Flying School badge

Rudder

Fin

Navigation light

K 3215

Elevator

Rudder cable

Tail plane

Tailwheel

Bracing strut

Valve rocker

Air cooling baffle

Magneto

Wing strut

Fuel tank

Throttle

Harness

Pilot's seat

Crankcase breather pipe

Directly driven propeller

Main front strut to engine mount

Limit of fuselage skin

Skid upper bracing strut

Rubber cord suspension

Turnbuckle

Ash skid

Axle

Skid rear strut

Lateral bracing strut

Rubber tire

Wheel rim

Wire wheel

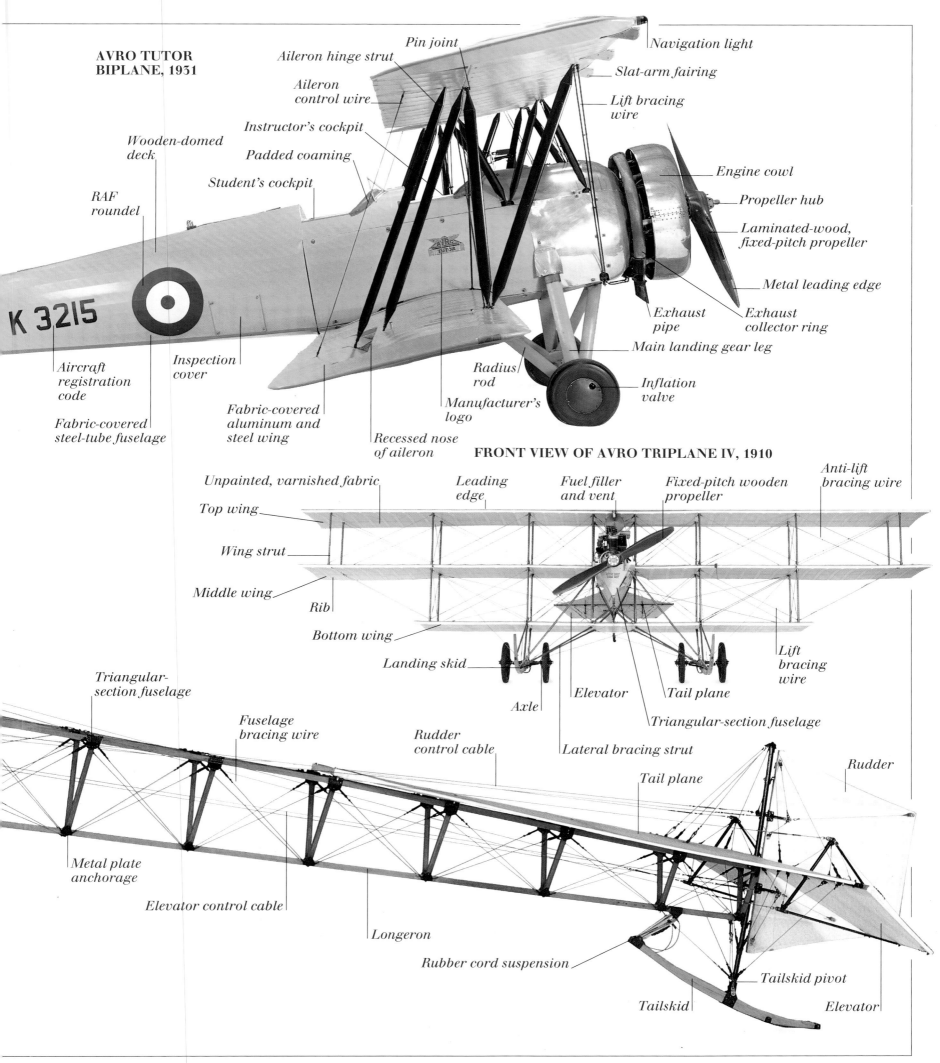

AVRO TUTOR BIPLANE, 1931

Pin joint

Aileron hinge strut

Navigation light

Slat-arm fairing

Aileron control wire

Lift bracing wire

Instructor's cockpit

Wooden-domed deck

Padded coaming

Student's cockpit

Engine cowl

Propeller hub

Laminated-wood, fixed-pitch propeller

RAF roundel

Metal leading edge

Exhaust pipe

Exhaust collector ring

Main landing gear leg

Radius rod

Inflation valve

Aircraft registration code

Inspection cover

Manufacturer's logo

Fabric-covered steel-tube fuselage

Fabric-covered aluminum and steel wing

Recessed nose of aileron

FRONT VIEW OF AVRO TRIPLANE IV, 1910

Unpainted, varnished fabric

Leading edge

Fuel filler and vent

Fixed-pitch wooden propeller

Anti-lift bracing wire

Top wing

Wing strut

Middle wing

Rib

Bottom wing

Landing skid

Axle

Elevator

Tail plane

Lift bracing wire

Triangular-section fuselage

Triangular-section fuselage

Fuselage bracing wire

Rudder control cable

Lateral bracing strut

Tail plane

Rudder

Metal plate anchorage

Elevator control cable

Longeron

Rubber cord suspension

Tailskid

Tailskid pivot

Elevator

World War I aircraft

FLYING HELMET

Wｈｅｎ Ｗｏｒｌｄ Ｗａｒ Ｉ ｓｔａｒｔｅｄ in 1914, the main purpose of military aircraft was reconnaissance. The British-built BE 2, of which the BE 2B was a variant, was well suited to this duty; it was very stable in flight, allowing the occupants to study the terrain, take photographs, and make notes. The BE 2 was also one of the first aircraft to drop bombs.

One of the biggest problems for aircraft designers during the war was mounting machine guns. On aircraft that had front-mounted propellers, the field of fire was restricted by the propeller and other parts of the aircraft. The problem was solved in 1915 by the Dutchman Anthony Fokker, who designed an interrupter gear that prevented a machine gun from firing when a propeller blade passed in front of the barrel. The German LVG CVI had a forward-firing gun to the right of the engine, as well as a rear-cockpit gun, and bombing capability. It was one of the most versatile aircraft of the war.

PORT WINGS FROM A BE 2B

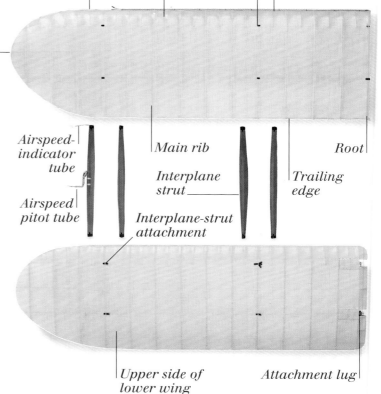

Intermediate leading-edge rib
Interplane-strut attachment
Airspeed-indicator tube
Leading edge
Wingtip
Airspeed-indicator tube
Main rib
Root
Interplane strut
Trailing edge
Airspeed pitot tube
Interplane-strut attachment
Upper side of lower wing
Attachment lug

BE 2B, 1914

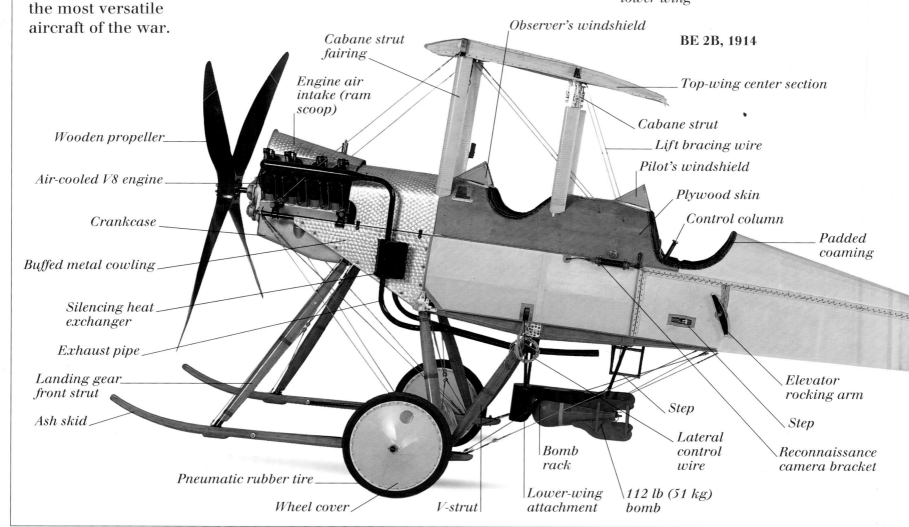

Cabane strut fairing
Observer's windshield
Engine air intake (ram scoop)
Top-wing center section
Cabane strut
Wooden propeller
Lift bracing wire
Air-cooled V8 engine
Pilot's windshield
Crankcase
Plywood skin
Control column
Buffed metal cowling
Padded coaming
Silencing heat exchanger
Exhaust pipe
Landing gear front strut
Elevator rocking arm
Ash skid
Step
Step
Bomb rack
Lateral control wire
Reconnaissance camera bracket
Pneumatic rubber tire
Wheel cover
V-strut
Lower-wing attachment
112 lb (51 kg) bomb

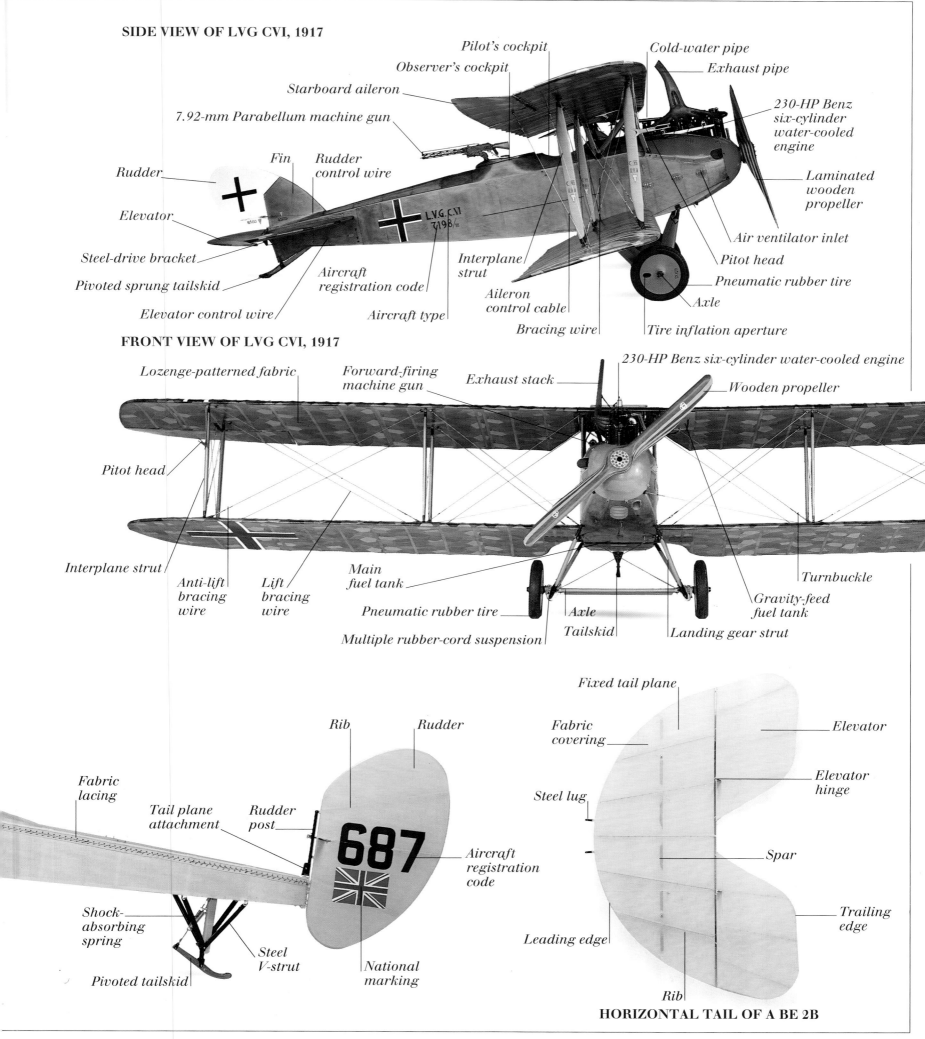

SIDE VIEW OF LVG CVI, 1917

Pilot's cockpit

Observer's cockpit

Cold-water pipe

Exhaust pipe

Starboard aileron

7.92-mm Parabellum machine gun

230-HP Benz six-cylinder water-cooled engine

Fin

Rudder
control wire

Rudder

Laminated wooden propeller

Elevator

Steel-drive bracket

Air ventilator inlet

Pivoted sprung tailskid

Pitot head

Aircraft registration code

Interplane strut

Pneumatic rubber tire

Elevator control wire

Aircraft type

Aileron control cable

Axle

Bracing wire

Tire inflation aperture

FRONT VIEW OF LVG CVI, 1917

Lozenge-patterned fabric

Forward-firing machine gun

Exhaust stack

230-HP Benz six-cylinder water-cooled engine

Wooden propeller

Pitot head

Interplane strut

Anti-lift bracing wire

Lift bracing wire

Main fuel tank

Turnbuckle

Gravity-feed fuel tank

Pneumatic rubber tire

Axle

Tailskid

Landing gear strut

Multiple rubber-cord suspension

Fixed tail plane

Fabric lacing

Fabric covering

Elevator

Rib

Rudder

Tail plane attachment

Rudder post

Steel lug

Elevator hinge

687

Aircraft registration code

Spar

Shock-absorbing spring

Steel V-strut

National marking

Leading edge

Trailing edge

Pivoted tailskid

Rib

HORIZONTAL TAIL OF A BE 2B

15

Early cockpits and instruments

THERMOCOUPLE AMMETER, c.1940

ONE OF THE FIRST FLIGHT instruments, the statoscope, was used in early balloon flights to indicate ascent and descent. The development of powered flight led to the introduction of cockpits and more instruments. Early cockpits had rudder pedals; a control column (for maneuvering); and flight, engine, and systems instruments. Flight instruments commonly included an airspeed indicator, altimeter (showing altitude), clinometer (showing tilt and pitch), and magnetic compass (for navigation). Engine instruments typically included an oil-pressure gauge, fuel-level gauge, tachometer (indicating engine speed), and a dual electric power indicator (showing electricity production and consumption). One of the earliest systems instruments was the flap indicator, which showed the position of the flaps on the wings.

Ascent scale
Suspension ring
Zero line
Opening to atmosphere
Descent scale
Indicator needle
Case containing aneroid capsule
Warning notice
Suspension cord

"WING SPRING" AIRSPEED INDICATOR, 1910

Pressure plate
Operating arm
Installation and maintenance instructions
Indicator bar
Indicator arm
Airspeed scale
Aluminum frame
Pivot
Coil spring
Spring-tension adjuster
Adjustment holes

Static air pressure head
Closed end
Mounting bracket
Open end
Dynamic air pressure head
Static air pressure tube
Airspeed scale in mph
Needle
Wooden panel
Outer casing
Dynamic air pressure tube

OGILVIE AIRSPEED INDICATOR, c.1918

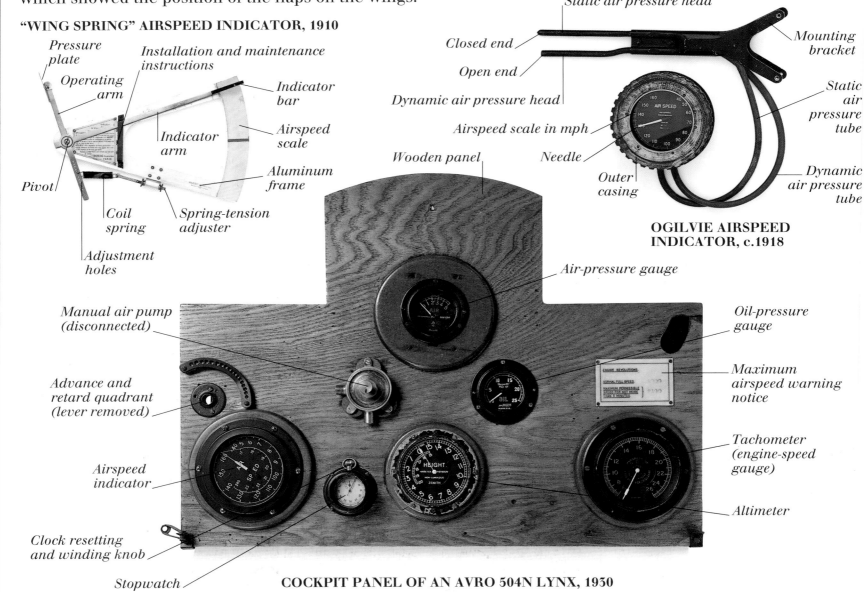

Manual air pump (disconnected)
Air-pressure gauge
Oil-pressure gauge
Advance and retard quadrant (lever removed)
Maximum airspeed warning notice
Airspeed indicator
Tachometer (engine-speed gauge)
Clock resetting and winding knob
Altimeter
Stopwatch

COCKPIT PANEL OF AN AVRO 504N LYNX, 1930

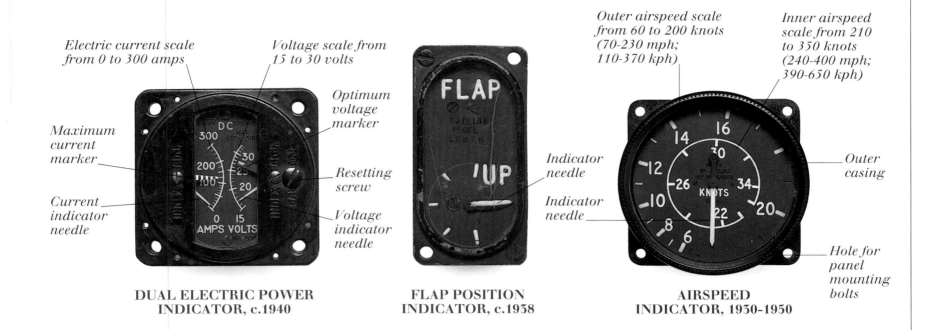

Electric current scale from 0 to 300 amps

Voltage scale from 15 to 30 volts

Maximum current marker

Optimum voltage marker

Current indicator needle

Resetting screw

Voltage indicator needle

DUAL ELECTRIC POWER INDICATOR, c.1940

Indicator needle

Indicator needle

FLAP POSITION INDICATOR, c.1938

Outer airspeed scale from 60 to 200 knots (70-230 mph; 110-370 kph)

Inner airspeed scale from 210 to 350 knots (240-400 mph; 390-650 kph)

Outer casing

Hole for panel mounting bolts

AIRSPEED INDICATOR, 1930-1950

COCKPIT OF A BRISTOL FIGHTER, 1917

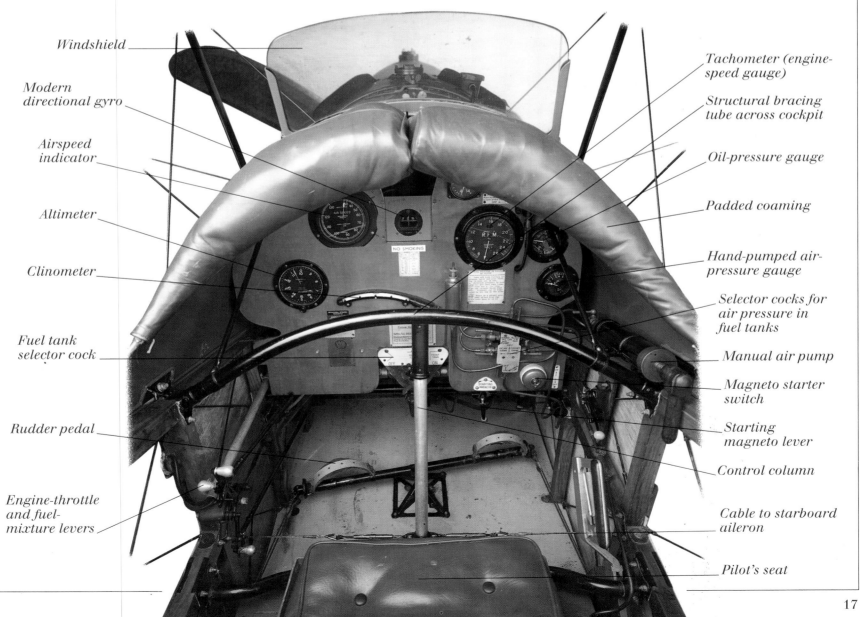

Windshield

Modern directional gyro

Airspeed indicator

Altimeter

Clinometer

Fuel tank selector cock

Rudder pedal

Engine-throttle and fuel-mixture levers

Tachometer (engine-speed gauge)

Structural bracing tube across cockpit

Oil-pressure gauge

Padded coaming

Hand-pumped air-pressure gauge

Selector cocks for air pressure in fuel tanks

Manual air pump

Magneto starter switch

Starting magneto lever

Control column

Cable to starboard aileron

Pilot's seat

Seaplanes and flying boats

SEAPLANES AND FLYING BOATS TAKE OFF from and land on water. On seaplanes only the floats touch the water, but on flying boats the fuselage itself is partly submerged. Modern seaplanes have two large floats. Some early seaplanes had an additional tail float, or a large central float balanced by small wingtip floats. Flying boats have a specially-shaped fuselage, similar to the hull of a ship, that runs easily across water. Like center-float seaplanes, they need stabilizing wingtip floats. A few early flying boats had twin hulls; others, instead of floats, had deep, stubby wings that rested on the water. Due to the lack of adequate runways, flying boats were widely used as passenger aircraft until the end of World War II. Both types of marine aircraft were also used for various military tasks, including dropping torpedoes, bombing, reconnaissance, and transport. Today they are used mainly for racing and for special purposes such as dumping water on forest fires.

SHORT S23 EMPIRE FLYING BOAT, 1936

VICKERS VIKING FLYING BOAT FUSELAGE, 1921

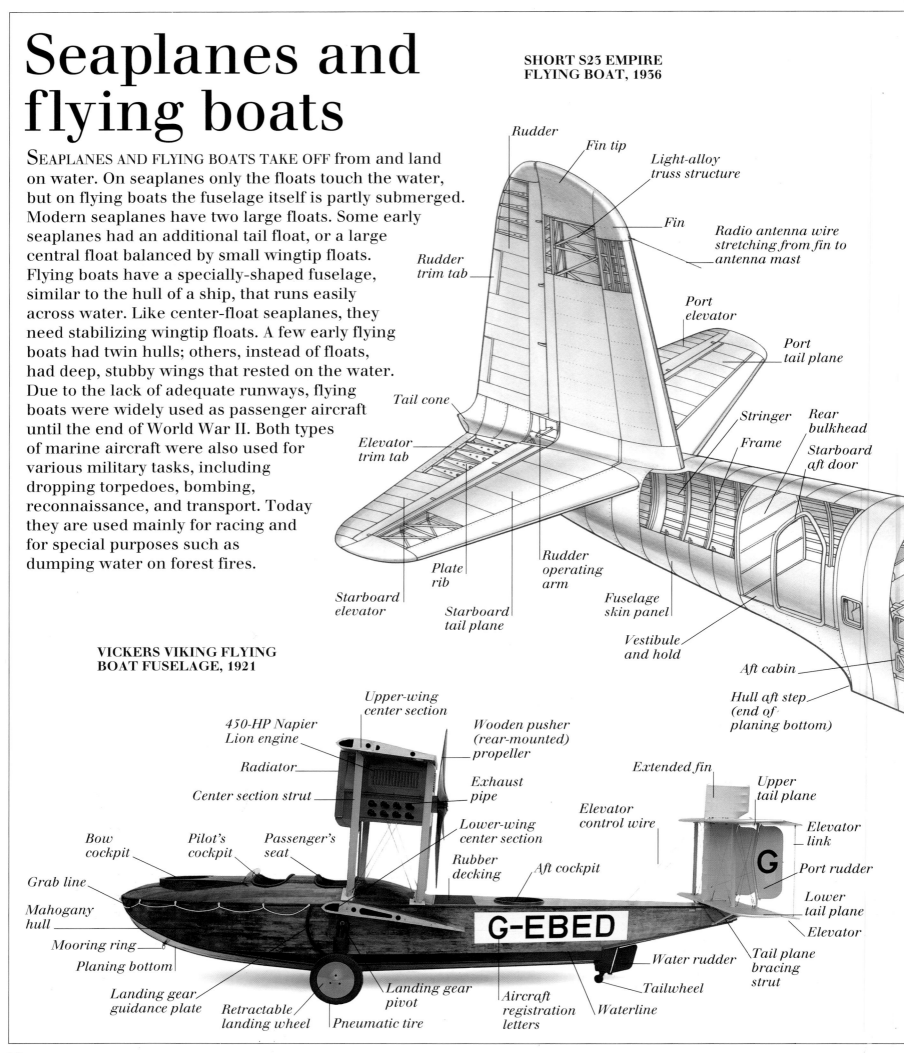

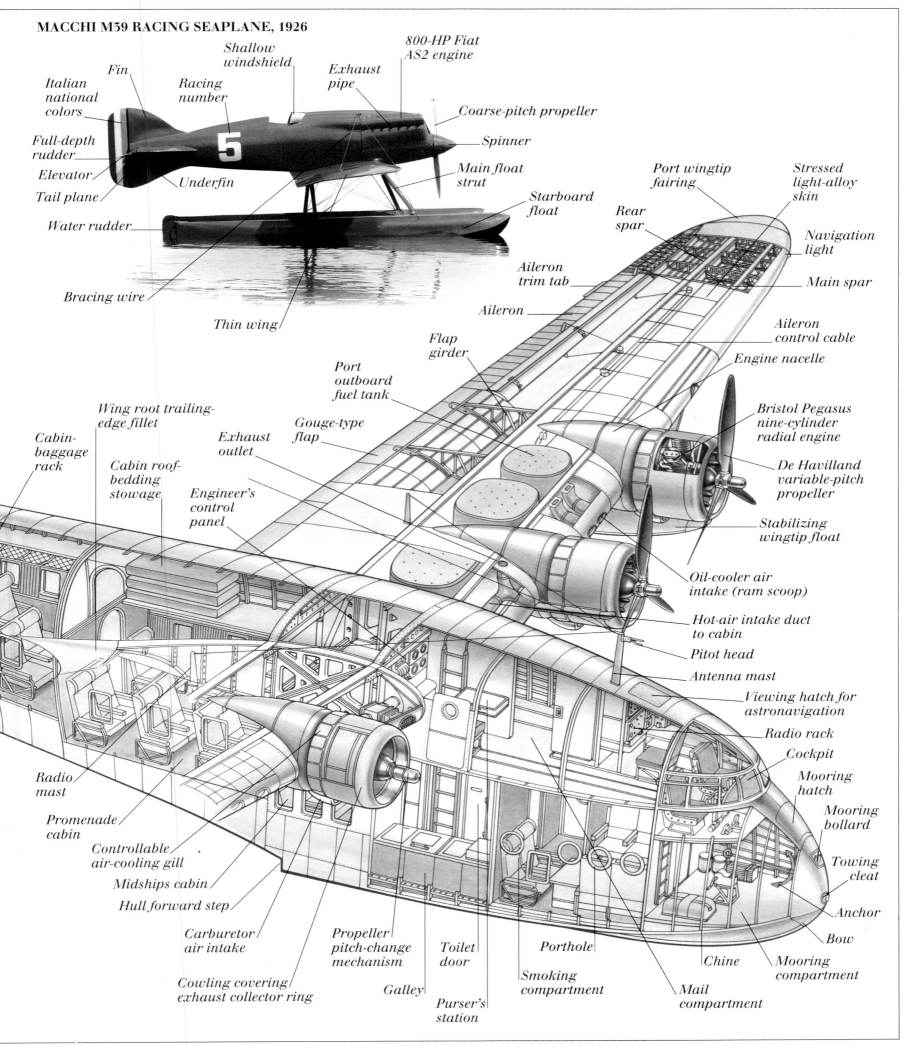

MACCHI M39 RACING SEAPLANE, 1926

Fin

Italian national colors

Shallow windshield

Racing number

Exhaust pipe

800-HP Fiat AS2 engine

Coarse-pitch propeller

Full-depth rudder

Spinner

Elevator

Tail plane

Underfin

Main float strut

Water rudder

Starboard float

Port wingtip fairing

Stressed light-alloy skin

Rear spar

Navigation light

Aileron trim tab

Main spar

Aileron

Aileron control cable

Bracing wire

Thin wing

Flap girder

Engine nacelle

Port outboard fuel tank

Bristol Pegasus nine-cylinder radial engine

Wing root trailing-edge fillet

Exhaust outlet

Gouge-type flap

De Havilland variable-pitch propeller

Cabin-baggage rack

Cabin roof-bedding stowage

Engineer's control panel

Stabilizing wingtip float

Oil-cooler air intake (ram scoop)

Hot-air intake duct to cabin

Pitot head

Antenna mast

Viewing hatch for astronavigation

Radio rack

Cockpit

Mooring hatch

Radio mast

Mooring bollard

Promenade cabin

Towing cleat

Controllable air-cooling gill

Anchor

Midships cabin

Bow

Hull forward step

Carburetor air intake

Propeller pitch-change mechanism

Toilet door

Porthole

Chine

Mooring compartment

Cowling covering exhaust collector ring

Galley

Purser's station

Smoking compartment

Mail compartment

19

Early passenger aircraft

UNTIL THE 1930s, most passenger aircraft were biplanes, with two pairs of wings and a wooden or metal framework covered with fabric or, sometimes, plywood. Such aircraft were restricted to low speeds and low altitudes because of the drag on their wings. Many had an open cockpit, situated behind or in front of an enclosed—but unpressurized—cabin that carried a maximum of 10 people. The passengers usually sat in wicker chairs that were not bolted to the floor, and the journey could be bumpy when flying through turbulence. Warm clothing, and earplugs to reduce the effects of prolonged noise, were often required. During the 1930s, powerful, streamlined, all-metal monoplanes, such as the Lockheed Electra shown here, became widespread. By 1939, the advent of pressurized cabins allowed fast flights at high altitudes, where there is less turbulence. Flying boats (see pp. 18-19) were still necessary on many routes until 1945 because of inadequate runways and the frequency of emergency sea landings. World War II, however, resulted in enough good runways being built for landplanes to become standard on all major airline routes.

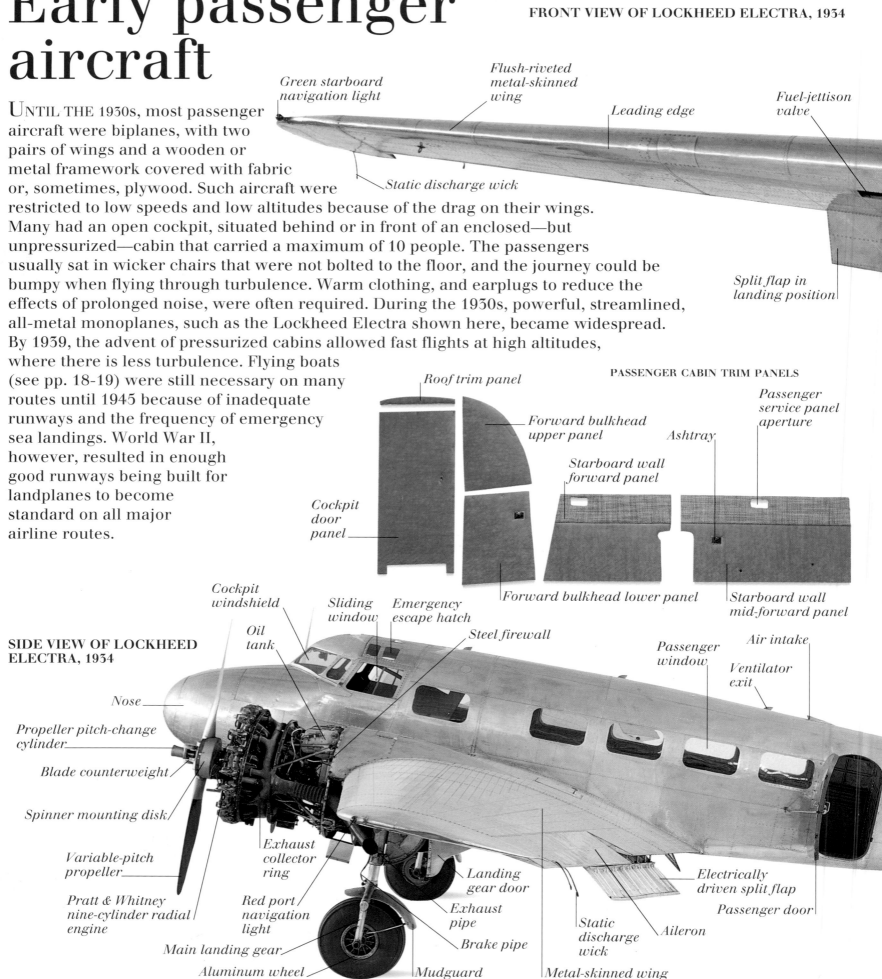

Green starboard navigation light

Flush-riveted metal-skinned wing

Leading edge

Fuel-jettison valve

Static discharge wick

Split flap in landing position

PASSENGER CABIN TRIM PANELS

Roof trim panel

Forward bulkhead upper panel

Passenger service panel aperture

Starboard wall forward panel

Ashtray

Cockpit door panel

Forward bulkhead lower panel

Starboard wall mid-forward panel

SIDE VIEW OF LOCKHEED ELECTRA, 1934

Cockpit windshield

Oil tank

Sliding window

Emergency escape hatch

Steel firewall

Passenger window

Air intake

Ventilator exit

Nose

Propeller pitch-change cylinder

Blade counterweight

Spinner mounting disk

Variable-pitch propeller

Pratt & Whitney nine-cylinder radial engine

Exhaust collector ring

Red port navigation light

Landing gear door

Exhaust pipe

Electrically driven split flap

Passenger door

Main landing gear

Brake pipe

Static discharge wick

Aileron

Aluminum wheel

Mudguard

Metal-skinned wing

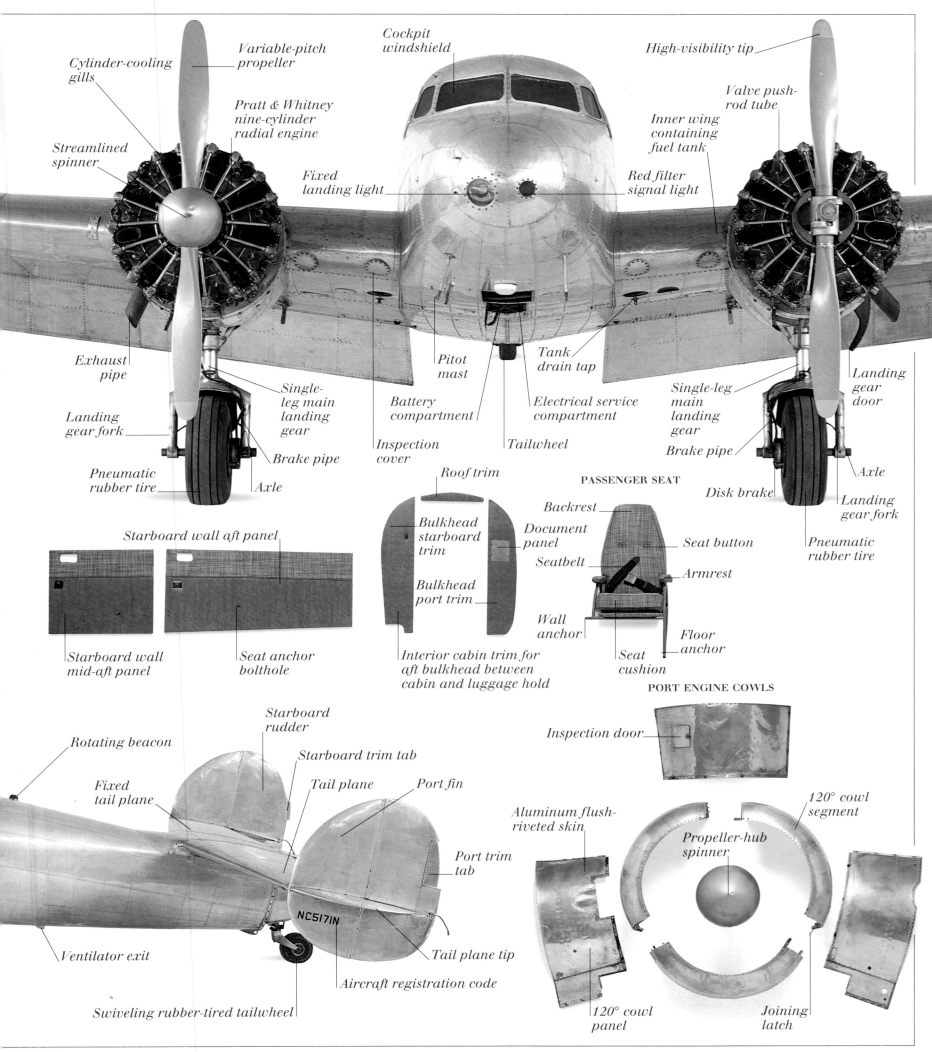

Cylinder-cooling gills

Variable-pitch propeller

Cockpit windshield

High-visibility tip

Streamlined spinner

Pratt & Whitney nine-cylinder radial engine

Valve push-rod tube

Inner wing containing fuel tank

Fixed landing light

Red filter signal light

Exhaust pipe

Single-leg main landing gear

Pitot mast

Tank drain tap

Single-leg main landing gear

Landing gear door

Landing gear fork

Battery compartment

Electrical service compartment

Brake pipe

Axle

Pneumatic rubber tire

Inspection cover

Tailwheel

Disk brake

Landing gear fork

Brake pipe

Axle

Pneumatic rubber tire

Starboard wall aft panel

Roof trim

PASSENGER SEAT

Backrest

Seat button

Bulkhead starboard trim

Document panel

Seatbelt

Armrest

Bulkhead port trim

Wall anchor

Floor anchor

Starboard wall mid-aft panel

Seat anchor bolthole

Interior cabin trim for aft bulkhead between cabin and luggage hold

Seat cushion

PORT ENGINE COWLS

Starboard rudder

Inspection door

Rotating beacon

Starboard trim tab

Fixed tail plane

Tail plane

Port fin

Aluminum flush-riveted skin

120° cowl segment

Port trim tab

Propeller-hub spinner

Ventilator exit

Tail plane tip

NC517IN

Aircraft registration code

Swiveling rubber-tired tailwheel

120° cowl panel

Joining latch

World War II aircraft

When World War II began in 1939, air forces had already replaced most of their fabric-skinned biplanes with all-metal stressed-skin monoplanes. Aircraft played a far greater role in military operations during World War II than ever before. The wide range of aircraft duties and the introduction of radar tracking and guidance systems put pressure on designers to improve aircraft performance. The main areas of improvement were speed, range, and engine power. Bombers became larger and more powerful—converting from two to four engines—in order to carry a heavier bomb load; the U.S. B-17 Flying Fortress could carry up to 6 tons of bombs over a distance of about 2,000 miles (3,200 km). Some aircraft increased their range by using drop tanks (fuel tanks that were jettisoned when empty to reduce drag). Fighters needed speed and maneuverability: the Hawker Tempest shown here had a maximum speed of 435 mph (700 kph) and was one of the few Allied aircraft capable of catching the German jet-powered V1 "flying bomb." By 1944, Britain had introduced its first turbojet-powered aircraft, the Gloster Meteor fighter, and Germany had introduced the fastest fighter in the world, the turbojet-powered Me 262, which had a maximum speed of 540 mph (868 kph).

STARBOARD ENGINE COWLINGS

- Radiator-access cowling
- Lower side cowling
- Upper side cowling
- Cowling fastener

PROPELLER

- High-visibility yellow tip
- Light-alloy propeller spinner
- Variable-pitch aluminum-alloy blade

COMPONENTS OF A HAWKER TEMPEST MARK V, c.1943

- Propeller governor
- 2,400-HP Napier Sabre 24-cylinder engine
- Cartridge starter
- Radiator header tank
- Propeller drive shaft
- Distributor
- Ejector exhaust
- Magneto
- Starter motor

- Engine top cowling
- Cowling fastener
- Upper side cowling
- Lower side cowling
- Radiator-access cowling

PORT ENGINE COWLINGS

SECTIONED B-17G FLYING FORTRESS BOMBER, c.1943

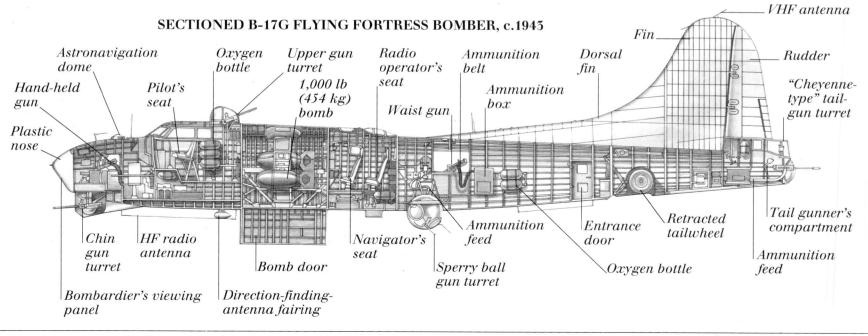

- Astronavigation dome
- Oxygen bottle
- Upper gun turret
- Radio operator's seat
- Ammunition belt
- Dorsal fin
- Fin
- VHF antenna
- Rudder
- Hand-held gun
- Pilot's seat
- 1,000 lb (454 kg) bomb
- Ammunition box
- "Cheyenne-type" tail-gun turret
- Plastic nose
- Waist gun
- Chin gun turret
- HF radio antenna
- Navigator's seat
- Ammunition feed
- Entrance door
- Retracted tailwheel
- Tail gunner's compartment
- Bombardier's viewing panel
- Direction-finding-antenna fairing
- Bomb door
- Sperry ball gun turret
- Oxygen bottle
- Ammunition feed

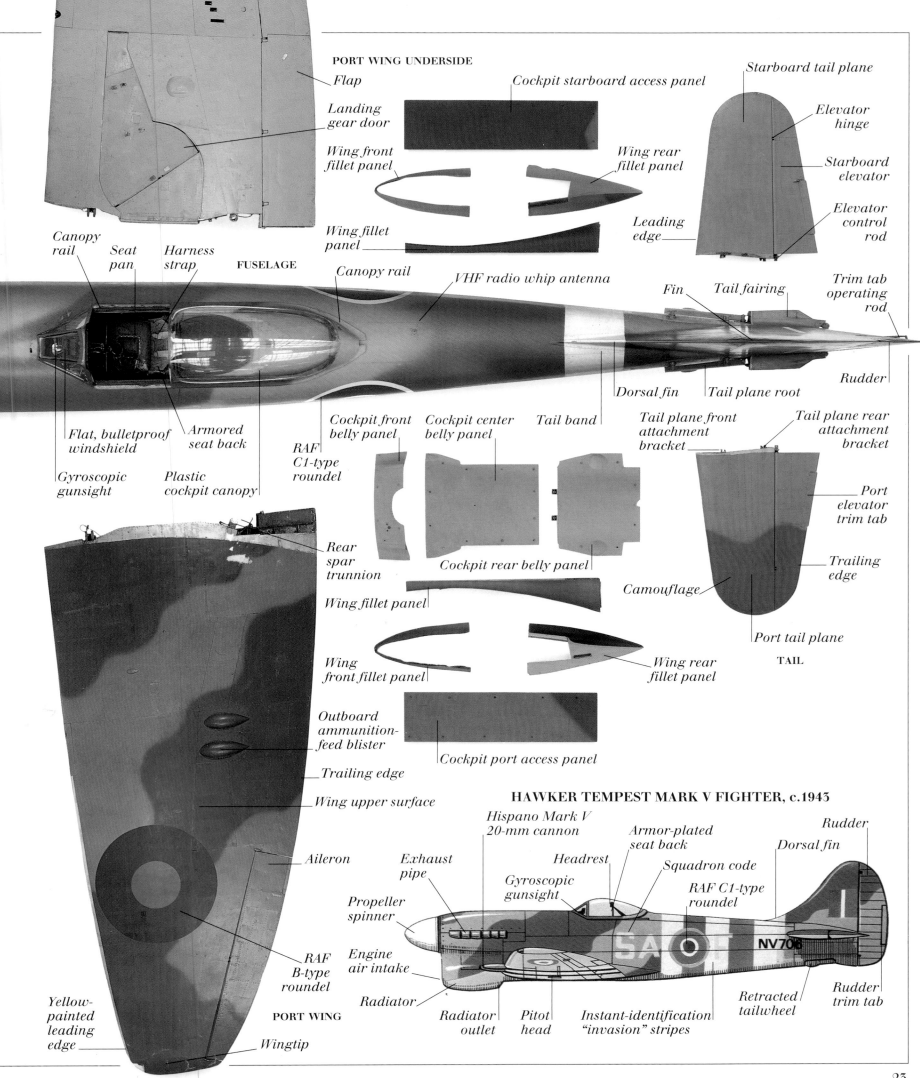

PORT WING UNDERSIDE

Flap

Cockpit starboard access panel

Starboard tail plane

Elevator hinge

Landing gear door

Wing front fillet panel

Wing rear fillet panel

Starboard elevator

Leading edge

Elevator control rod

Wing fillet panel

Canopy rail

Seat pan

Harness strap

FUSELAGE

Canopy rail

VHF radio whip antenna

Fin

Tail fairing

Trim tab operating rod

Dorsal fin

Tail plane root

Rudder

Flat, bulletproof windshield

Armored seat back

RAF C1-type roundel

Cockpit front belly panel

Cockpit center belly panel

Tail band

Tail plane front attachment bracket

Tail plane rear attachment bracket

Gyroscopic gunsight

Plastic cockpit canopy

Port elevator trim tab

Rear spar trunnion

Cockpit rear belly panel

Camouflage

Trailing edge

Wing fillet panel

Wing front fillet panel

Wing rear fillet panel

Port tail plane

TAIL

Outboard ammunition-feed blister

Cockpit port access panel

Trailing edge

Wing upper surface

HAWKER TEMPEST MARK V FIGHTER, c.1943

Aileron

Hispano Mark V 20-mm cannon

Armor-plated seat back

Rudder

Exhaust pipe

Headrest

Squadron code

Dorsal fin

Gyroscopic gunsight

RAF C1-type roundel

Propeller spinner

RAF B-type roundel

Engine air intake

Radiator

Yellow-painted leading edge

PORT WING

Radiator outlet

Pitot head

Instant-identification "invasion" stripes

Retracted tailwheel

Rudder trim tab

Wingtip

23

Early piston aircraft engines

GASOLINE-DRIVEN PISTON ENGINES were used in the first powered flights. The engine used in the 1903 Wright Flyer (see pp. 8-9) for the first recorded powered flight had four water-cooled cylinders that lay horizontally side by side. The Wright brothers had built their own engine and, although it worked, it was very crude. For instance, it had an ignition system that created a spark by pulling apart two pieces of metal in each cylinder. In 1907, the French Seguin brothers built the first rotary engine, the Gnome. Its five cylinders were arranged around a stationary crankshaft like the spokes of a wheel and spun around the crankshaft to turn the propeller. However, the spinning motion of rotary engines could cause aircraft to pull to one side, and so by 1918 these engines were being replaced by two other types. One type had water-cooled cylinders arranged in a single line (in-line) or in a V-shape (like the V12 Kestrel shown here). The other was the air-cooled radial engine, which was similar to the rotary engine but had a spinning crankshaft to turn the propeller while the cylinders remained stationary.

110-HP LE RHÔNE 9B ROTARY ENGINE, 1914

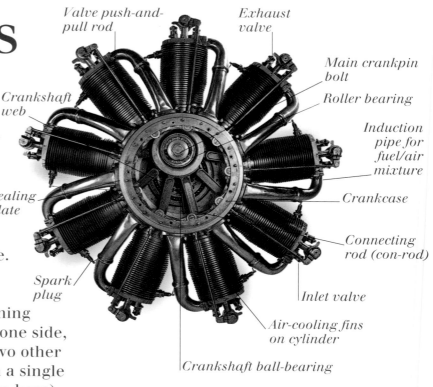

- Valve push-and-pull rod
- Exhaust valve
- Main crankpin bolt
- Crankshaft web
- Roller bearing
- Induction pipe for fuel/air mixture
- Sealing plate
- Crankcase
- Connecting rod (con-rod)
- Spark plug
- Inlet valve
- Air-cooling fins on cylinder
- Crankshaft ball-bearing

CYLINDER ASSEMBLY OF A GNOME MONOSOUPAPE 100-HP ROTARY ENGINE, 1914

- Tappet roller retaining pin
- Valve lever
- Valve-lever fulcrum pin
- Valve spring
- Valve housing cage
- Push-rod
- Inlet and exhaust valve
- Tappet adjuster lock nut
- Air-cooling fins
- Spark plug
- Fuel transfer port
- Spark-plug aperture
- Cylinder barrel
- Gas-tight piston ring
- Piston
- Compression ring
- Small-end bearing
- Gudgeon pin aperture
- Connecting rod (con-rod)
- Oil-feed pipe
- Wrist pin bearing

ARMSTRONG SIDDELEY TIGER 14-CYLINDER RADIAL ENGINE, 1931

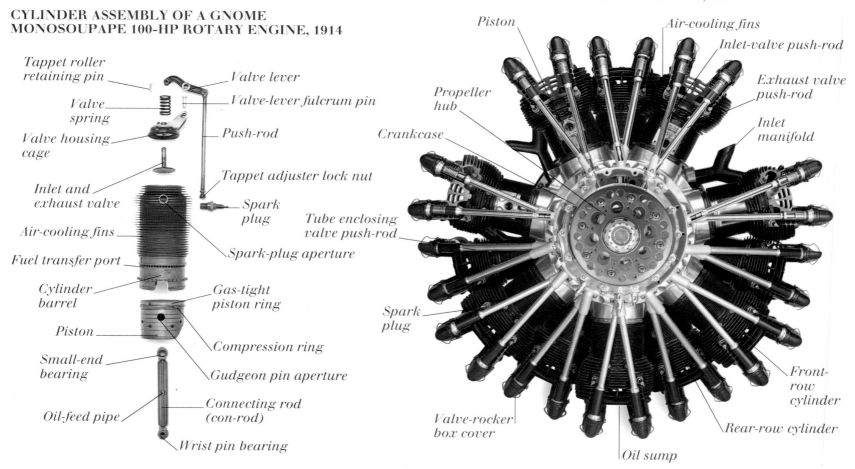

- Piston
- Air-cooling fins
- Inlet-valve push-rod
- Propeller hub
- Exhaust valve push-rod
- Crankcase
- Inlet manifold
- Tube enclosing valve push-rod
- Spark plug
- Front-row cylinder
- Valve-rocker box cover
- Rear-row cylinder
- Oil sump

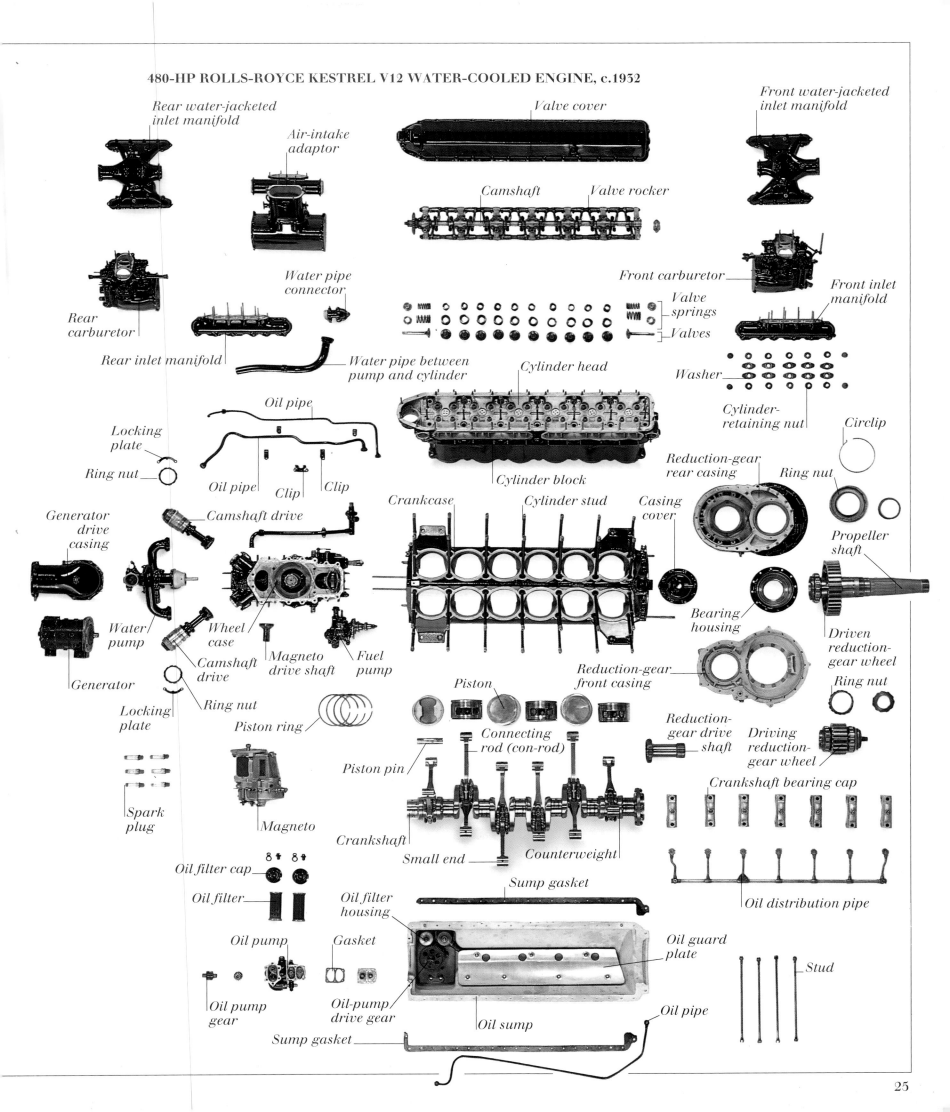

480-HP ROLLS-ROYCE KESTREL V12 WATER-COOLED ENGINE, c.1952

Rear water-jacketed inlet manifold

Air-intake adaptor

Valve cover

Front water-jacketed inlet manifold

Camshaft

Valve rocker

Front carburetor

Front inlet manifold

Rear carburetor

Water pipe connector

Valve springs

Valves

Rear inlet manifold

Water pipe between pump and cylinder

Cylinder head

Washer

Cylinder-retaining nut

Oil pipe

Locking plate

Ring nut

Oil pipe

Clip

Clip

Cylinder block

Circlip

Reduction-gear rear casing

Ring nut

Crankcase

Cylinder stud

Casing cover

Propeller shaft

Generator drive casing

Camshaft drive

Bearing housing

Driven reduction-gear wheel

Water pump

Wheel case

Camshaft drive

Magneto drive shaft

Fuel pump

Reduction-gear front casing

Ring nut

Generator

Ring nut

Piston

Reduction-gear drive shaft

Driving reduction-gear wheel

Locking plate

Piston ring

Connecting rod (con-rod)

Crankshaft bearing cap

Spark plug

Piston pin

Magneto

Crankshaft

Small end

Counterweight

Oil distribution pipe

Oil filter cap

Oil filter

Oil filter housing

Sump gasket

Oil guard plate

Oil pump

Gasket

Stud

Oil pump gear

Oil-pump drive gear

Oil sump

Oil pipe

Sump gasket

Modern piston aircraft engines

MID WEST TWO-STROKE, THREE-CYLINDER ENGINE

PISTON ENGINES today are used mainly to power the vast numbers of light aircraft and ultralights, as well as crop sprayers and crop dusters, small helicopters, and fire-bombers (which dump water on large fires). Virtually all heavier aircraft are now powered by jet engines. Modern piston aircraft engines work on the same basic principles as the engine used by the Wright brothers in the first powered flight in 1903. However, today's engines are more sophisticated than earlier engines. For example, modern aircraft engines may use a two-stroke or a four-stroke combustion cycle; they may have from one to nine air- or liquid-cooled cylinders, which may be arranged horizontally, in-line, in V formation or radially; and they may drive the aircraft's propeller either directly or through a reduction gearbox. One of the more unconventional types of modern aircraft engine is the rotary engine shown here, which has a trilobate (three-sided) rotor spinning in a chamber shaped like a fat figure-eight.

MID WEST 75-HP TWO-STROKE, THREE-CYLINDER ENGINE

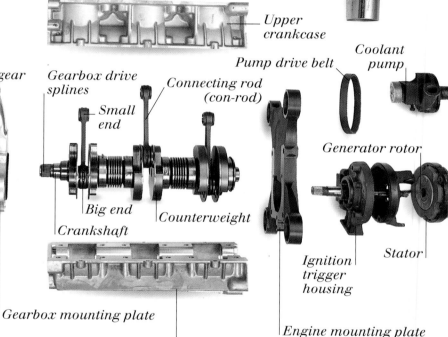

Spark plug

Coolant outlet

Cylinder head

Piston

Cylinder barrel

Exhaust manifold

Exhaust port

Cylinder liner

Upper crankcase

Reduction gearbox

Driven gear

Gearbox drive splines

Connecting rod (con-rod)

Coolant pump

Pump drive belt

Propeller drive flange

Small end

Generator rotor

Torsional vibration damper

Sprag clutch

Big end

Counterweight

Crankshaft

Ignition trigger housing

Stator

Gearbox mounting plate

Engine mounting plate

Lower crankcase

ROTOR AND HOUSINGS OF A MID WEST SINGLE-ROTOR ENGINE

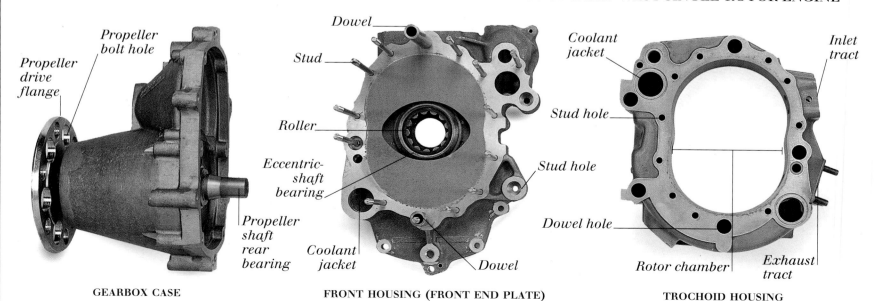

Propeller bolt hole

Propeller drive flange

Dowel

Stud

Coolant jacket

Inlet tract

Roller

Stud hole

Eccentric-shaft bearing

Stud hole

Propeller shaft rear bearing

Coolant jacket

Dowel

Dowel hole

Rotor chamber

Exhaust tract

GEARBOX CASE

FRONT HOUSING (FRONT END PLATE)

TROCHOID HOUSING

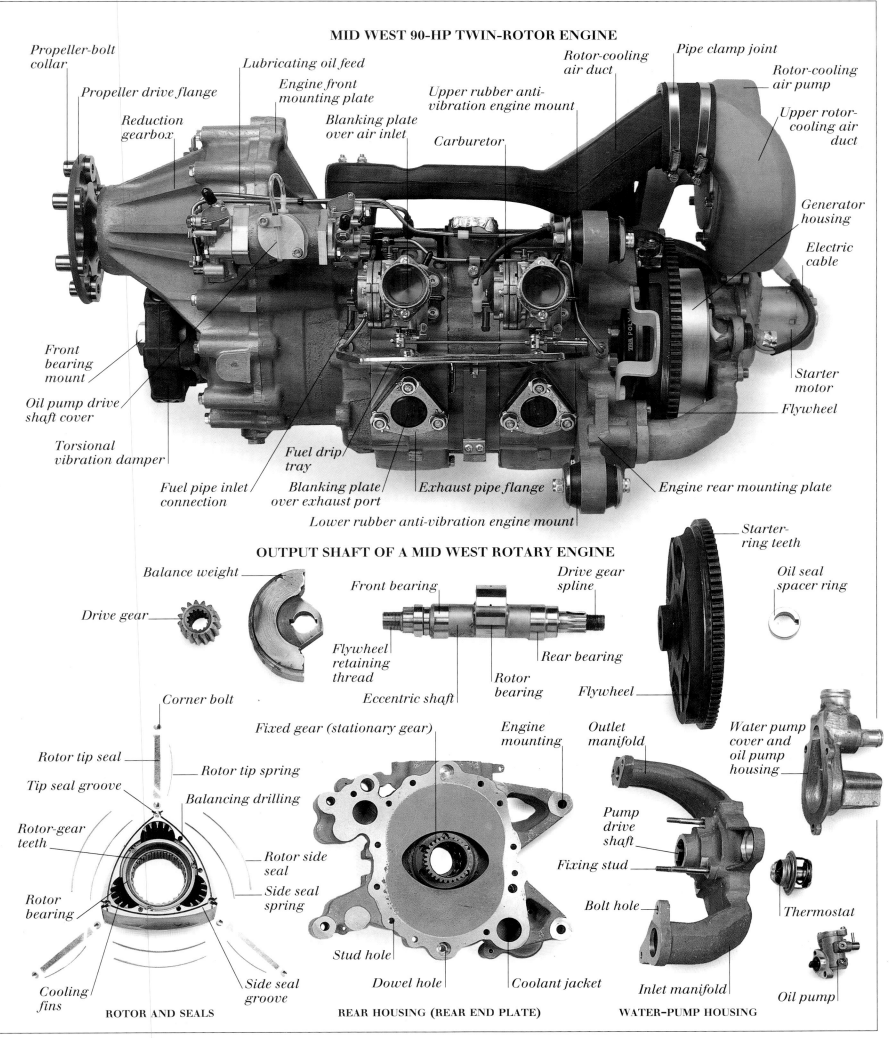

MID WEST 90-HP TWIN-ROTOR ENGINE

Propeller-bolt collar

Propeller drive flange

Reduction gearbox

Lubricating oil feed

Engine front mounting plate

Blanking plate over air inlet

Upper rubber anti-vibration engine mount

Carburetor

Rotor-cooling air duct

Pipe clamp joint

Rotor-cooling air pump

Upper rotor-cooling air duct

Generator housing

Electric cable

Front bearing mount

Oil pump drive shaft cover

Torsional vibration damper

Fuel pipe inlet connection

Fuel drip tray

Blanking plate over exhaust port

Exhaust pipe flange

Starter motor

Flywheel

Engine rear mounting plate

Lower rubber anti-vibration engine mount

OUTPUT SHAFT OF A MID WEST ROTARY ENGINE

Balance weight

Drive gear

Front bearing

Drive gear spline

Starter-ring teeth

Oil seal spacer ring

Flywheel retaining thread

Eccentric shaft

Rotor bearing

Rear bearing

Flywheel

Corner bolt

Rotor tip seal

Tip seal groove

Rotor tip spring

Balancing drilling

Fixed gear (stationary gear)

Engine mounting

Outlet manifold

Water pump cover and oil pump housing

Rotor-gear teeth

Rotor side seal

Pump drive shaft

Rotor bearing

Side seal spring

Fixing stud

Cooling fins

Side seal groove

Stud hole

Dowel hole

Coolant jacket

Bolt hole

Inlet manifold

Thermostat

Oil pump

ROTOR AND SEALS

REAR HOUSING (REAR END PLATE)

WATER-PUMP HOUSING

27

Wings

ALL AIRCRAFT EXCEPT BALLOONS AND AIRSHIPS rely on wings to fly. Even the blades of helicopters are basically rotating wings. The airflow over wing surfaces generates the lifting force necessary for flight. Wings are also crucial in maneuvering. Early wings, made from wood and fabric, were warped (twisted) by wires for banking and turning. Later wings used ailerons (hinged flaps on the trailing, or rear, edge) for banking and turning. Subsequent developments were flaps and slats. Flaps, on a wing's trailing edge, are moved down to increase lift during takeoff, climbing, and descent and to increase lift and drag during the landing approach. Slats, on the leading, or forward, edge, move forward to help prevent the aircraft from stalling. The Handley Page Gugnunc shown here was one of the first aircraft to combine all three features. Modern wings are metal-framed, with a skin made of metal or of a composite material such as carbon fiber. Wings on large aircraft may carry fuel tanks, engines, and retractable landing gear.

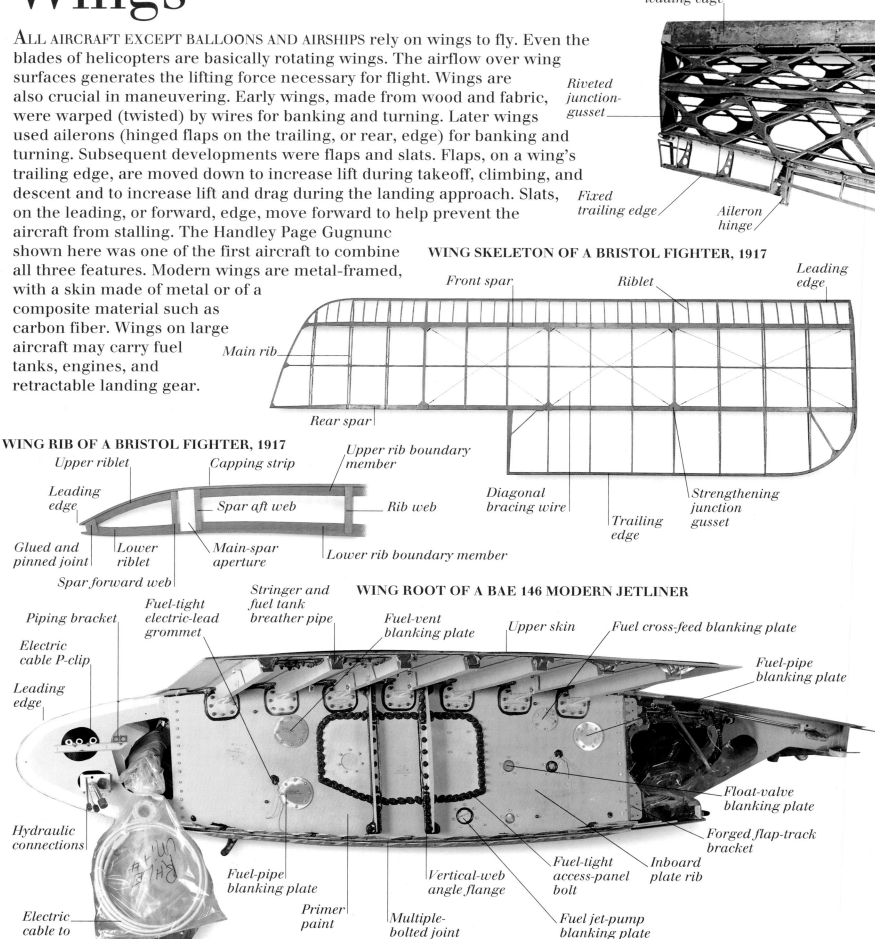

Aluminum-skinned leading edge

Riveted junction-gusset

Fixed trailing edge

Aileron hinge

WING SKELETON OF A BRISTOL FIGHTER, 1917

Front spar

Riblet

Leading edge

Main rib

Rear spar

Diagonal bracing wire

Strengthening junction gusset

Trailing edge

WING RIB OF A BRISTOL FIGHTER, 1917

Upper riblet

Capping strip

Upper rib boundary member

Leading edge

Spar aft web

Rib web

Glued and pinned joint

Lower riblet

Main-spar aperture

Lower rib boundary member

Spar forward web

WING ROOT OF A BAE 146 MODERN JETLINER

Piping bracket

Fuel-tight electric-lead grommet

Stringer and fuel tank breather pipe

Fuel-vent blanking plate

Upper skin

Fuel cross-feed blanking plate

Electric cable P-clip

Fuel-pipe blanking plate

Leading edge

Hydraulic connections

Float-valve blanking plate

Forged flap-track bracket

Electric cable to engines

Fuel-pipe blanking plate

Primer paint

Multiple-bolted joint

Vertical-web angle flange

Fuel-tight access-panel bolt

Fuel jet-pump blanking plate

Inboard plate rib

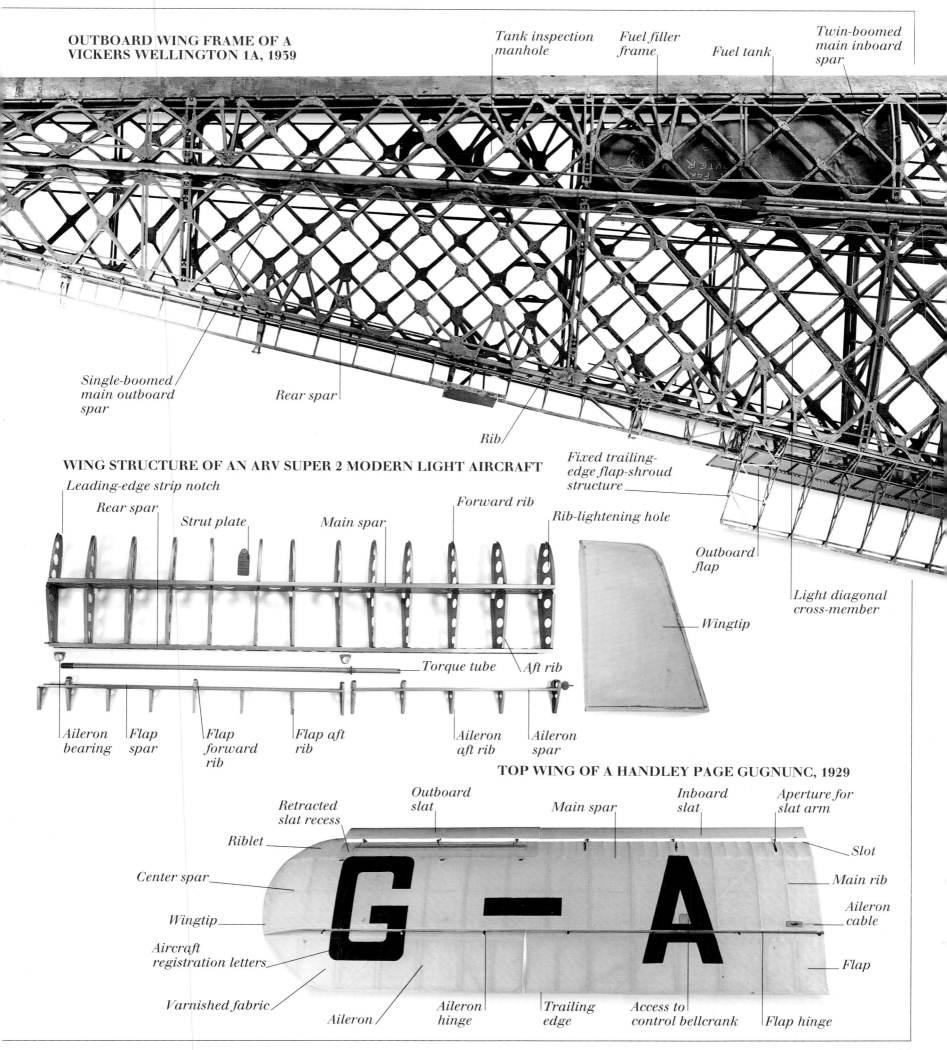

OUTBOARD WING FRAME OF A VICKERS WELLINGTON 1A, 1939

Tank inspection manhole

Fuel filler frame

Fuel tank

Twin-boomed main inboard spar

Single-boomed main outboard spar

Rear spar

Rib

WING STRUCTURE OF AN ARV SUPER 2 MODERN LIGHT AIRCRAFT

Leading-edge strip notch

Rear spar

Strut plate

Main spar

Forward rib

Rib-lightening hole

Fixed trailing-edge flap-shroud structure

Outboard flap

Light diagonal cross-member

Wingtip

Torque tube

Aft rib

Aileron bearing

Flap spar

Flap forward rib

Flap aft rib

Aileron aft rib

Aileron spar

TOP WING OF A HANDLEY PAGE GUGNUNC, 1929

Retracted slat recess

Outboard slat

Main spar

Inboard slat

Aperture for slat arm

Riblet

Slot

Center spar

Main rib

Wingtip

Aileron cable

Aircraft registration letters

Flap

Varnished fabric

Aileron

Aileron hinge

Trailing edge

Access to control bellcrank

Flap hinge

Fuselage

THE FUSELAGE IS THE MAIN BODY of an aircraft. The earliest airplanes did not have a fuselage (see pp. 8-9) but wooden-framed, fabric-skinned fuselages were soon adopted; in some of these early aircraft the skin covered only the nose and cockpit. During the 1920s and 1930s, most aircraft had steel fuselage frames covered with a metal skin or with metal and wooden panels. High-speed aircraft required an all-metal fuselage frame with a flush-riveted skin to produce a streamlined surface. The Vickers Wellington shown here has an unusual fuselage frame consisting of small curved rods riveted together to form a geodetic mesh. Pressurized jetliner fuselages, introduced in the 1940s, must maintain normal air pressure inside the aircraft so that the passengers can breathe while the aircraft is flying at high altitudes, where the external air pressure is extremely low. Such fuselages must withstand the stresses of expansion and contraction under varying external air pressures while remaining completely airtight.

PRESSURIZED FUSELAGE OF A MODERN JETLINER

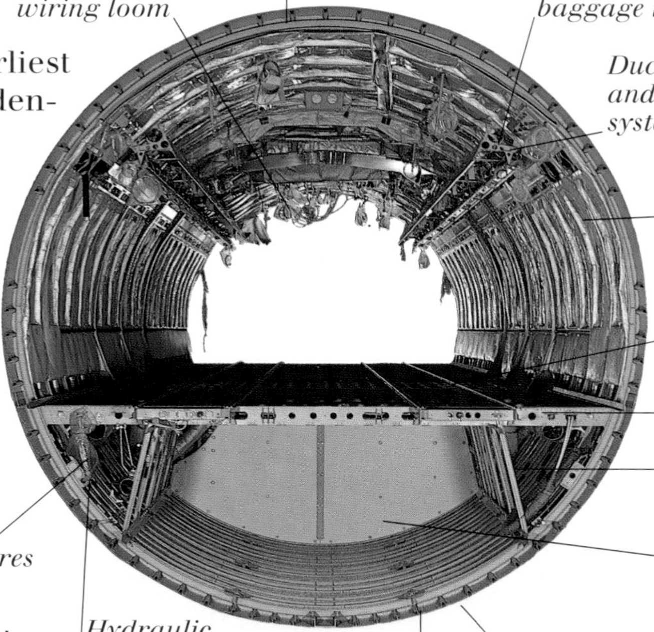

Electrical wiring loom

Metal frame

Bracket for overhead baggage lockers

Duct for electrical and air-conditioning systems

Reflective insulating foil

Seat rail

Transverse floor beam

Floor strut

Freight and baggage hold

Electrical control wires

Hydraulic control line

Bonded stringer

Aluminum-alloy skin

FUSELAGE OF A HAWKER HART TRAINER, 1933

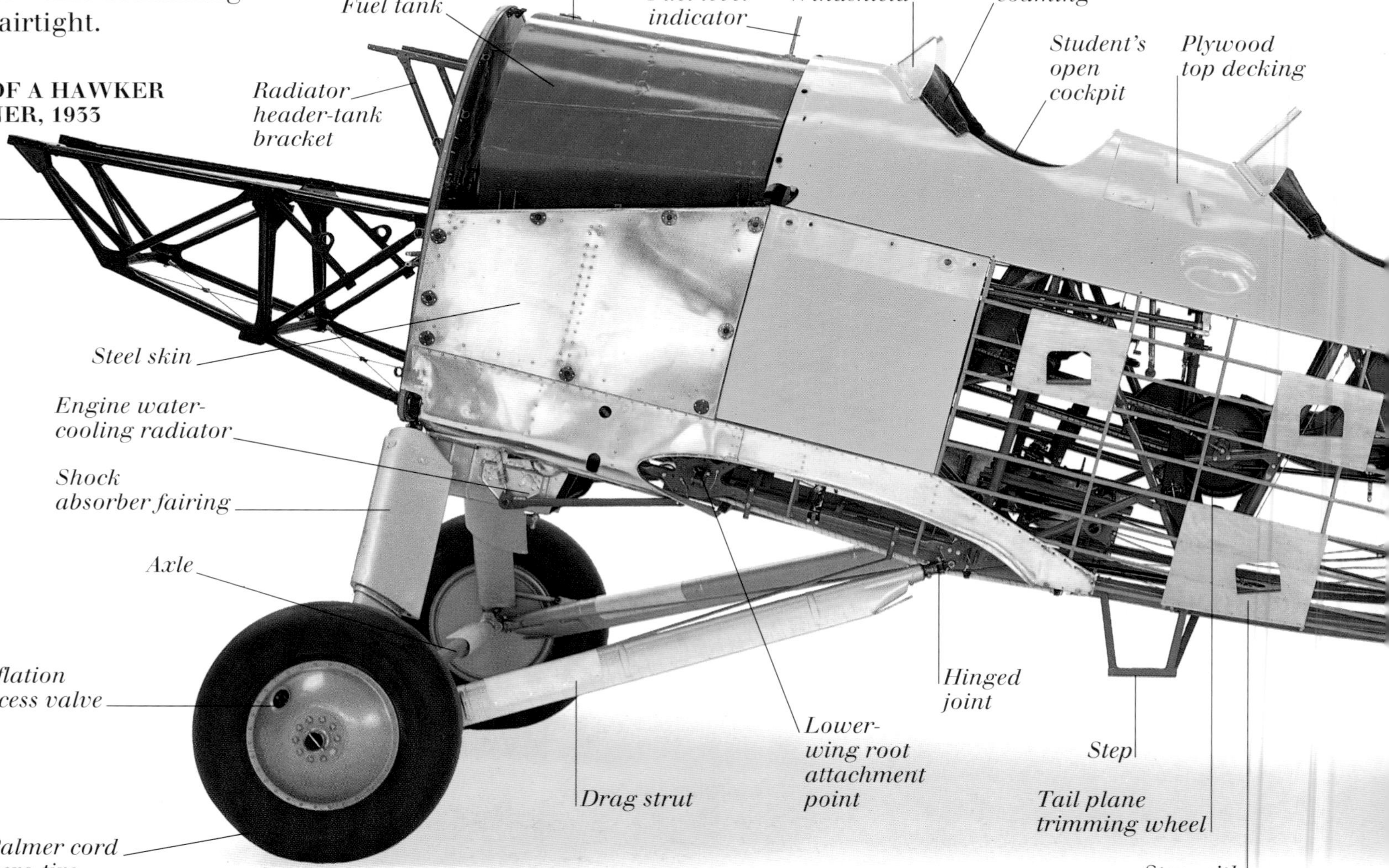

Fuel filler cap

Fuel tank

Fuel level indicator

Windshield

Padded coaming

Student's open cockpit

Plywood top decking

Radiator header-tank bracket

Engine cradle

Steel skin

Engine water-cooling radiator

Shock absorber fairing

Axle

Inflation access valve

Palmer cord aero-tire

Drag strut

Lower-wing root attachment point

Hinged joint

Step

Tail plane trimming wheel

Step with plywood reinforcement

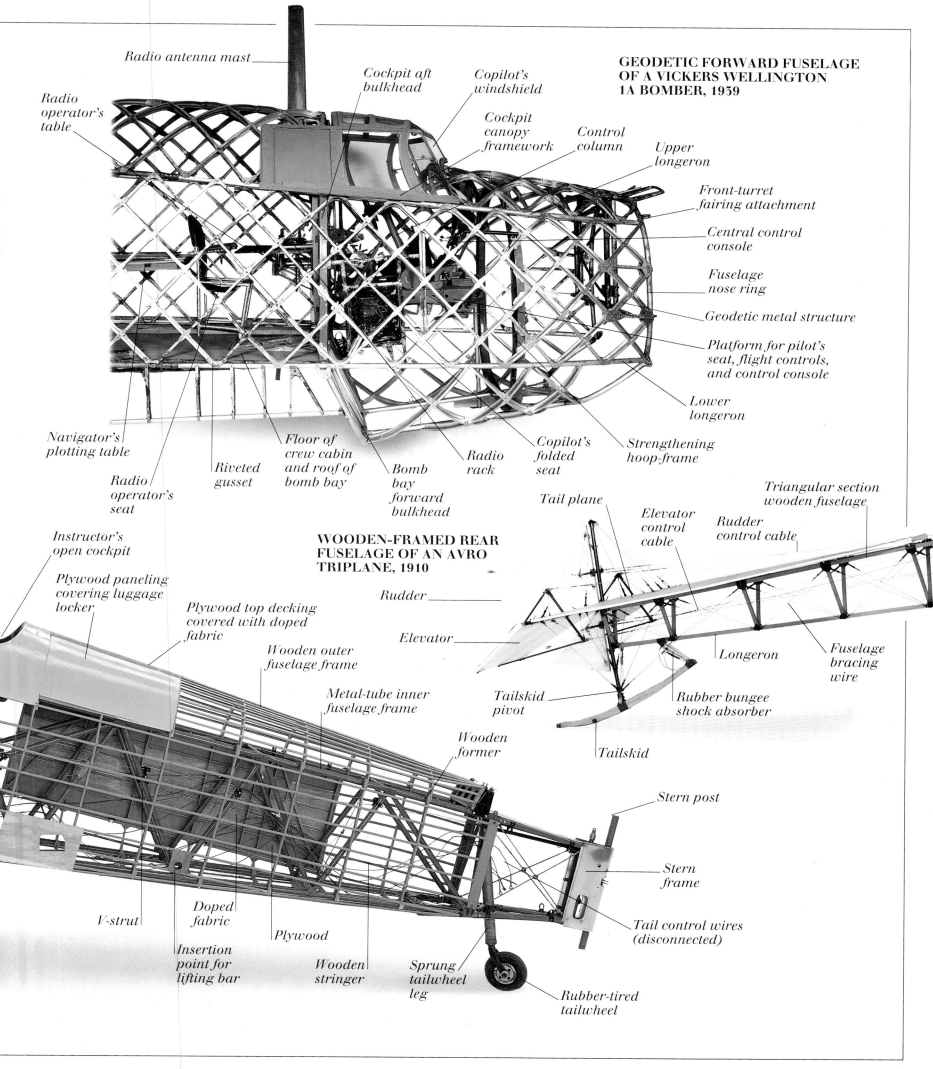

Radio antenna mast

Radio operator's table

GEODETIC FORWARD FUSELAGE OF A VICKERS WELLINGTON 1A BOMBER, 1939

Cockpit aft bulkhead

Copilot's windshield

Cockpit canopy framework

Control column

Upper longeron

Front-turret fairing attachment

Central control console

Fuselage nose ring

Geodetic metal structure

Platform for pilot's seat, flight controls, and control console

Lower longeron

Strengthening hoop-frame

Navigator's plotting table

Radio operator's seat

Riveted gusset

Floor of crew cabin and roof of bomb bay

Bomb bay forward bulkhead

Radio rack

Copilot's folded seat

Tail plane

Elevator control cable

Rudder control cable

Triangular section wooden fuselage

WOODEN-FRAMED REAR FUSELAGE OF AN AVRO TRIPLANE, 1910

Rudder

Elevator

Longeron

Fuselage bracing wire

Instructor's open cockpit

Plywood paneling covering luggage locker

Plywood top decking covered with doped fabric

Wooden outer fuselage frame

Metal-tube inner fuselage frame

Wooden former

Tailskid pivot

Tailskid

Rubber bungee shock absorber

Stern post

Stern frame

V-strut

Doped fabric

Plywood

Wooden stringer

Insertion point for lifting bar

Sprung tailwheel leg

Rubber-tired tailwheel

Tail control wires (disconnected)

Landing gear

HELICOPTER LANDING SKIDS

LANDING GEAR ALLOWS AIRCRAFT to move on the ground, and absorbs shocks to enable smooth landing and takeoff. The earliest aircraft used wire wheels, wooden struts to brace them to the fuselage, and, usually, a simple skid beneath the tail. Rubber bungees (elasticated cords) absorbed shocks when landing and long, curved skids at the front prevented the aircraft from overturning. As aircraft became heavier and faster, pressed-steel wheels, metal legs, sprung shock absorbers, and fluid dampers came into use. During the 1930s, retractable landing gear was introduced to reduce drag during flight. With the introduction of large, heavy jetliners, multiwheel landing gear was adopted. This landing gear had a bogie (pivoting trolley) with up to eight wheels at the bottom of each leg. At the same time, nose landing gear, not used since 1914, became widely adopted, enabling pilots to make safer and smoother landings.

COMPONENTS OF MODERN MAIN LANDING GEAR

Retraction actuator attachment

Forward bearing

Aircraft attachment pin

Retraction actuator

Drag strut

Upper side stay

Upper cardan joint

Lock link

Piston rod

Center joint

Upper cardan pin

Lower cardan lug

Main shock strut

Lock link actuator

Down lock-spring

Torque link attachment

Lower side stay

Shock absorber outer tube containing hydraulic cylinder

Shock absorber stroke

Lower cardan joint

Lower cardan pin

Right wheel bearing

Left wheel bearing

Torque link

Brake torque flange

Axle

MODERN TWIN-WHEEL MAIN LANDING GEAR

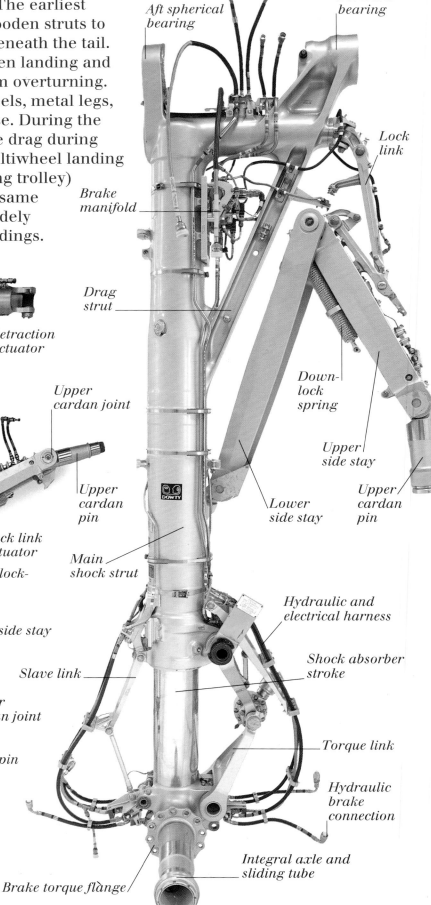

Aft spherical bearing

Forward bearing

Lock link

Brake manifold

Drag strut

Down-lock spring

Upper side stay

Upper cardan pin

Lower side stay

Main shock strut

Upper cardan pin

Hydraulic and electrical harness

Shock absorber stroke

Slave link

Torque link

Left wheel bearing

Hydraulic brake connection

Integral axle and sliding tube

Brake torque flange

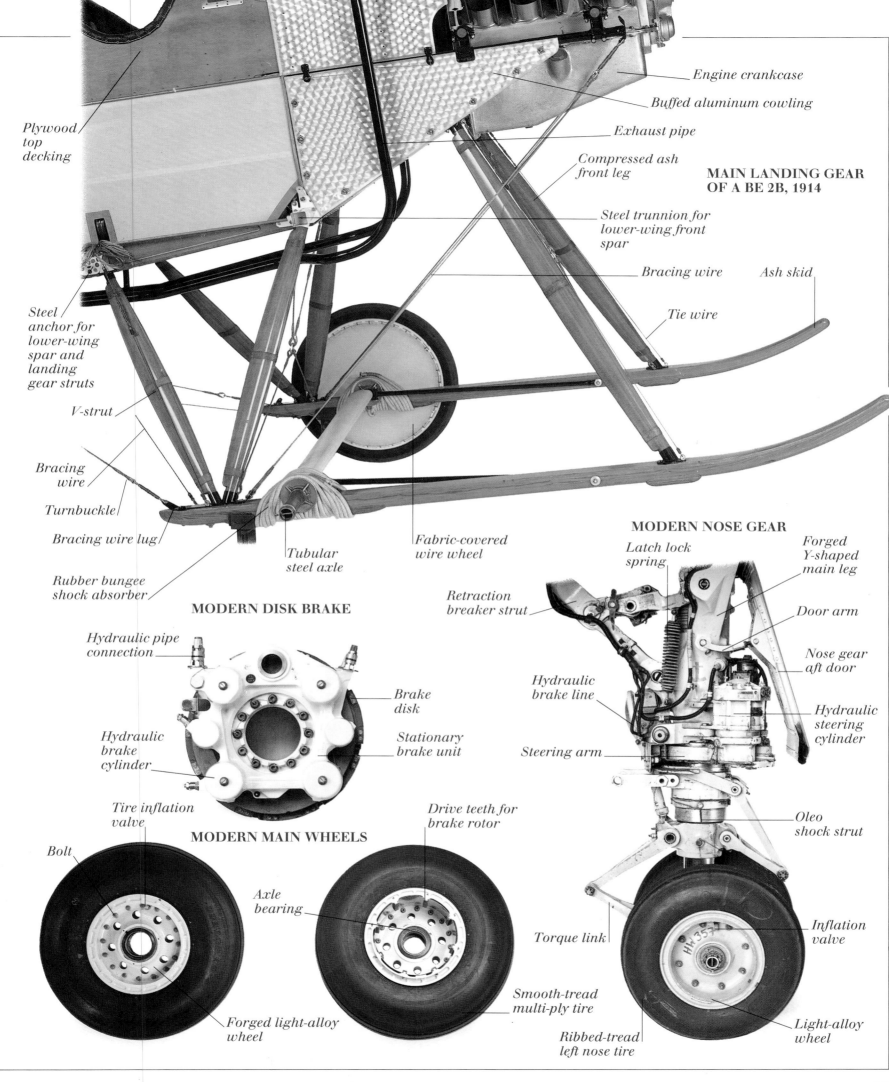

Plywood top decking

Steel anchor for lower-wing spar and landing gear struts

V-strut

Bracing wire

Turnbuckle

Bracing wire lug

Rubber bungee shock absorber

Tubular steel axle

Fabric-covered wire wheel

Engine crankcase

Buffed aluminum cowling

Exhaust pipe

Compressed ash front leg

MAIN LANDING GEAR OF A BE 2B, 1914

Steel trunnion for lower-wing front spar

Bracing wire

Ash skid

Tie wire

MODERN DISK BRAKE

Hydraulic pipe connection

Hydraulic brake cylinder

Brake disk

Stationary brake unit

Tire inflation valve

MODERN MAIN WHEELS

Bolt

Axle bearing

Drive teeth for brake rotor

Forged light-alloy wheel

Smooth-tread multi-ply tire

Ribbed-tread left nose tire

MODERN NOSE GEAR

Latch lock spring

Retraction breaker strut

Hydraulic brake line

Steering arm

Forged Y-shaped main leg

Door arm

Nose gear aft door

Hydraulic steering cylinder

Oleo shock strut

Torque link

Inflation valve

Light-alloy wheel

33

Modern jetliners 1

BAE 146 JETLINER

MODERN JETLINERS HAVE ENABLED ordinary people to travel to places where once only the wealthy could afford to go. Compared with the first jetliners (which were introduced in the 1940s), modern jetliners are much quieter, burn fuel more efficiently, and produce less air pollution. These advances are largely due to the replacement of turbojet engines with turbofan engines (see pp. 42-43). The greater power of turbofan engines at low speeds enables modern jetliners to carry more fuel and passengers than turbojet aircraft; a modern Boeing 747-400 (popularly known as a "jumbo jet") can fly 400 people for 8,500 miles (13,700 km) without needing to refuel. Jetliners fly at high altitudes, typically cruising at 26,000-36,000 ft (8,000-11,000 m), where they can use fuel efficiently and usually avoid bad weather. The pilot always controls the aircraft during takeoff and landing, but at other times the aircraft is usually controlled by an autopilot. Autopilots are complex onboard mechanisms that detect deviations from an aircraft's route and make appropriate adjustments to the flight controls. Flight decks are also equipped with radar that warns pilots of approaching hazards, such as mountain ranges, bad weather, and other aircraft.

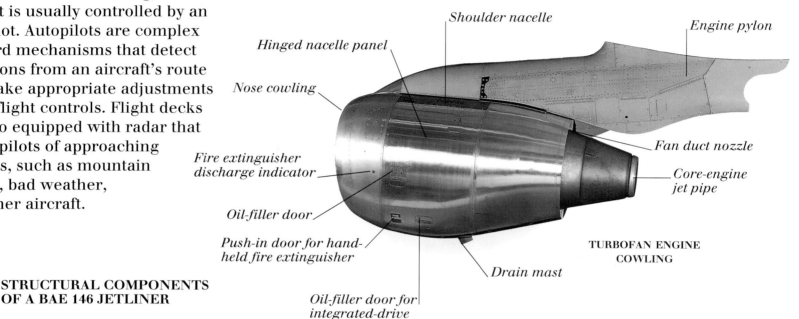

Shoulder nacelle

Engine pylon

Hinged nacelle panel

Nose cowling

Fan duct nozzle

Fire extinguisher discharge indicator

Core-engine jet pipe

Oil-filler door

Push-in door for hand-held fire extinguisher

Drain mast

TURBOFAN ENGINE COWLING

Oil-filler door for integrated-drive generator

STRUCTURAL COMPONENTS OF A BAE 146 JETLINER

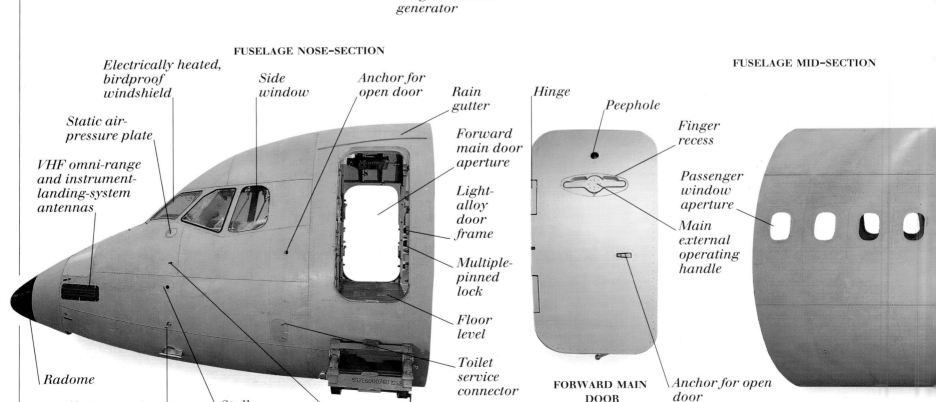

FUSELAGE NOSE-SECTION

FUSELAGE MID-SECTION

Electrically heated, birdproof windshield

Side window

Anchor for open door

Rain gutter

Hinge

Peephole

Finger recess

Static air-pressure plate

Forward main door aperture

Passenger window aperture

VHF omni-range and instrument-landing-system antennas

Light-alloy door frame

Main external operating handle

Multiple-pinned lock

Floor level

Radome

Toilet service connector

Anchor for open door

FORWARD MAIN DOOR

Air temperature probe

Stall-warning vane

Pitot head for dynamic air pressure

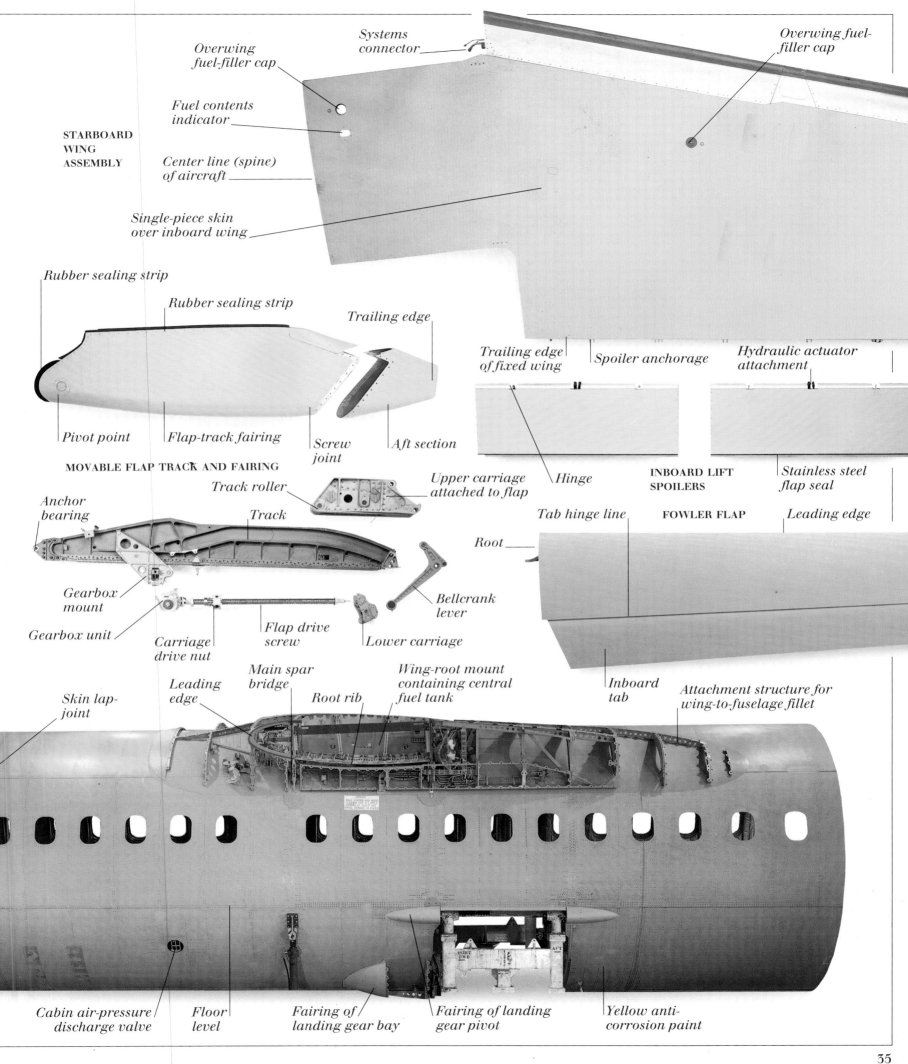

STARBOARD WING ASSEMBLY

Overwing fuel-filler cap

Systems connector

Overwing fuel-filler cap

Fuel contents indicator

Center line (spine) of aircraft

Single-piece skin over inboard wing

Rubber sealing strip

Rubber sealing strip

Trailing edge

Trailing edge of fixed wing

Spoiler anchorage

Hydraulic actuator attachment

Pivot point

Flap-track fairing

Screw joint

Aft section

Hinge

INBOARD LIFT SPOILERS

Stainless steel flap seal

MOVABLE FLAP TRACK AND FAIRING

Upper carriage attached to flap

Track roller

Track

FOWLER FLAP

Tab hinge line

Leading edge

Anchor bearing

Root

Gearbox mount

Gearbox unit

Carriage drive nut

Flap drive screw

Lower carriage

Bellcrank lever

Main spar bridge

Wing-root mount containing central fuel tank

Leading edge

Root rib

Skin lap-joint

Inboard tab

Attachment structure for wing-to-fuselage fillet

Cabin air-pressure discharge valve

Floor level

Fairing of landing gear bay

Fairing of landing gear pivot

Yellow anti-corrosion paint

35

Modern jetliners 2

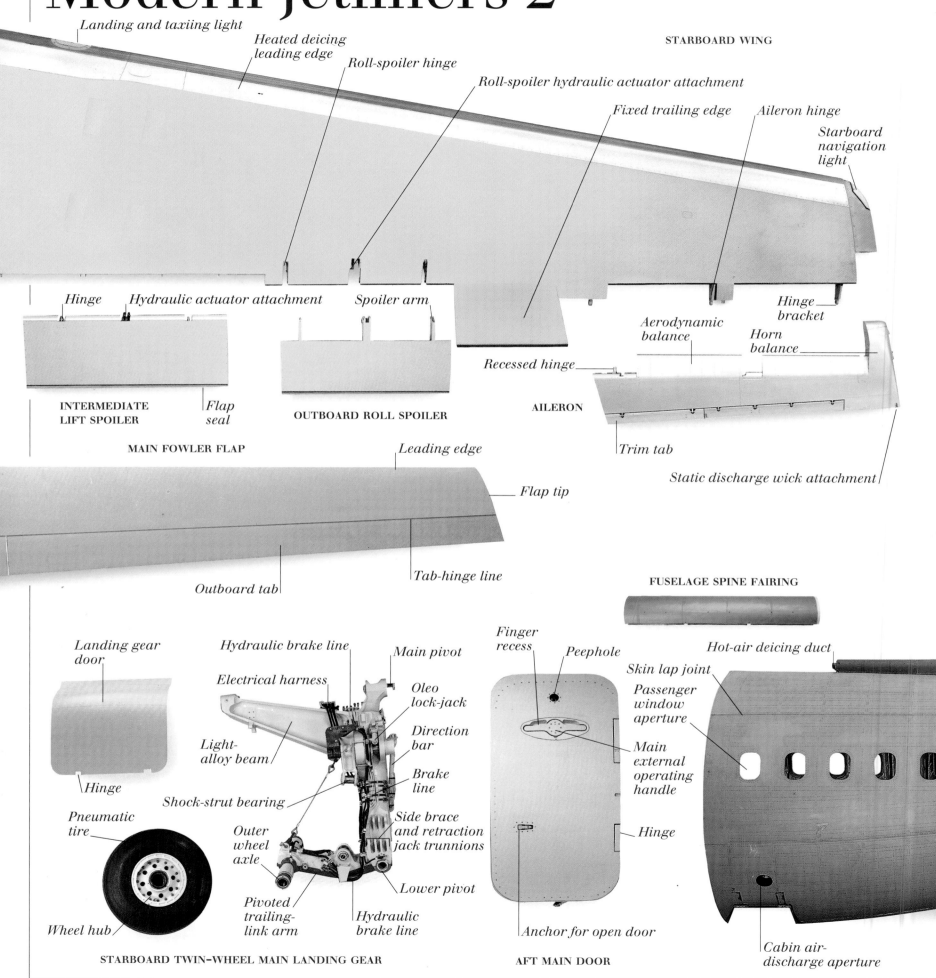

Landing and taxiing light

Heated deicing leading edge

Roll-spoiler hinge

STARBOARD WING

Roll-spoiler hydraulic actuator attachment

Fixed trailing edge

Aileron hinge

Starboard navigation light

Hinge

Hydraulic actuator attachment

Spoiler arm

Aerodynamic balance

Hinge bracket

Horn balance

Recessed hinge

INTERMEDIATE LIFT SPOILER

Flap seal

OUTBOARD ROLL SPOILER

AILERON

Trim tab

MAIN FOWLER FLAP

Leading edge

Static discharge wick attachment

Flap tip

FUSELAGE SPINE FAIRING

Outboard tab

Tab-hinge line

Finger recess

Peephole

Hot-air deicing duct

Landing gear door

Hydraulic brake line

Main pivot

Skin lap joint

Electrical harness

Oleo lock-jack

Passenger window aperture

Light-alloy beam

Direction bar

Main external operating handle

Brake line

Shock-strut bearing

Pneumatic tire

Outer wheel axle

Side brace and retraction jack trunnions

Hinge

Hinge

Wheel hub

Pivoted trailing-link arm

Hydraulic brake line

Lower pivot

Anchor for open door

Cabin air-discharge aperture

STARBOARD TWIN-WHEEL MAIN LANDING GEAR

AFT MAIN DOOR

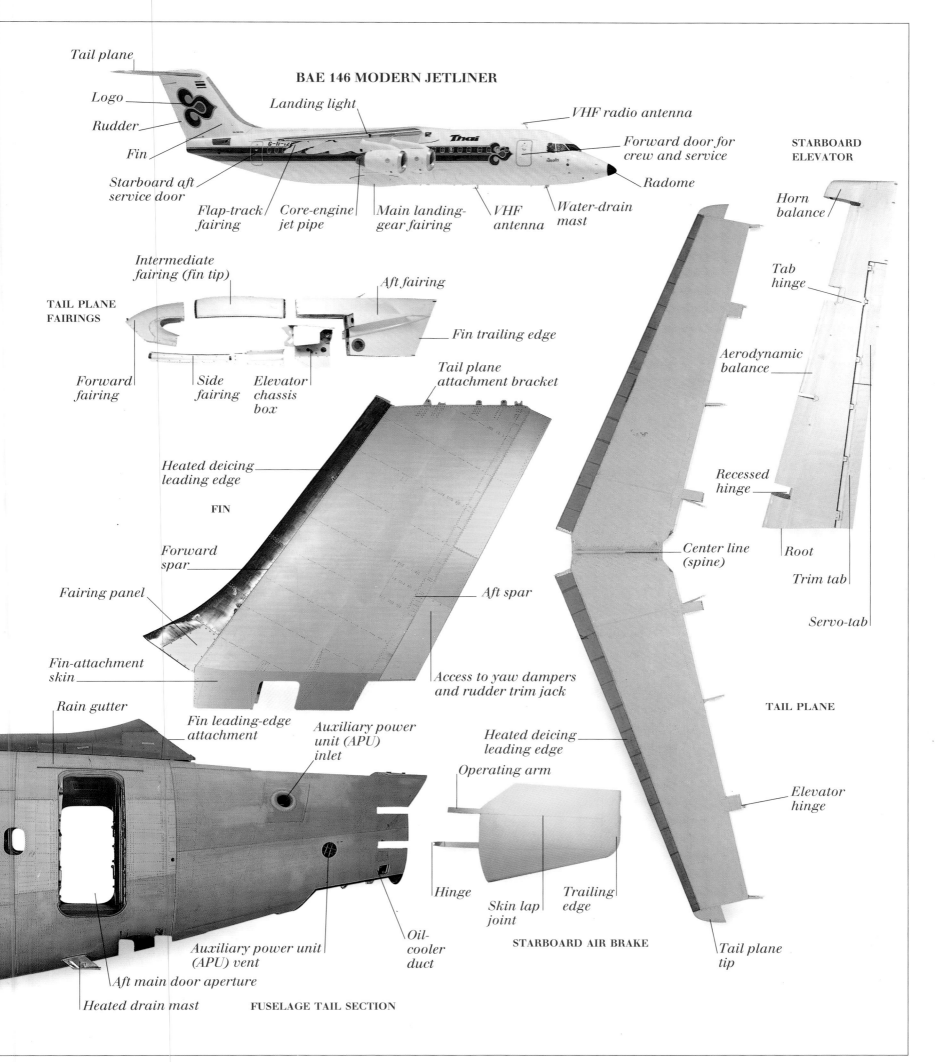

BAE 146 MODERN JETLINER

Tail plane

Logo

Rudder

Fin

Starboard aft service door

Flap-track fairing

Core-engine jet pipe

Landing light

Main landing-gear fairing

VHF antenna

VHF radio antenna

Forward door for crew and service

Radome

Water-drain mast

STARBOARD ELEVATOR

Horn balance

Tab hinge

Aerodynamic balance

Recessed hinge

Root

Trim tab

Servo-tab

TAIL PLANE FAIRINGS

Intermediate fairing (fin tip)

Aft fairing

Fin trailing edge

Forward fairing

Side fairing

Elevator chassis box

Tail plane attachment bracket

Heated deicing leading edge

FIN

Forward spar

Fairing panel

Aft spar

Fin-attachment skin

Access to yaw dampers and rudder trim jack

Center line (spine)

TAIL PLANE

Rain gutter

Fin leading-edge attachment

Auxiliary power unit (APU) inlet

Heated deicing leading edge

Operating arm

Elevator hinge

Auxiliary power unit (APU) vent

Oil-cooler duct

Hinge

Skin lap joint

Trailing edge

Tail plane tip

Aft main door aperture

Heated drain mast

FUSELAGE TAIL SECTION

STARBOARD AIR BRAKE

Elevator hinge

Modern cockpits

THE COCKPITS OF MODERN AIRCRAFT contain many data-display instruments, as well as aircraft controls. All modern airplanes have engine instruments (which indicate data such as fuel levels and power) and flight instruments. There are four main flight instruments: the altimeter, artificial horizon, airspeed indicator, and directional gyroscope. Many aircraft have two additional flight instruments: a turn-and-slip indicator and a vertical speed indicator. Some aircraft also have systems instruments, which indicate data such as the position of flaps and ailerons and cabin pressure. In the most up-to-date cockpits, data are presented on electronic display screens. The most important screens are the primary flight display (which simultaneously shows data from all the flight instruments), and the navigational display (which combines the functions of compass, radar screen, and map).

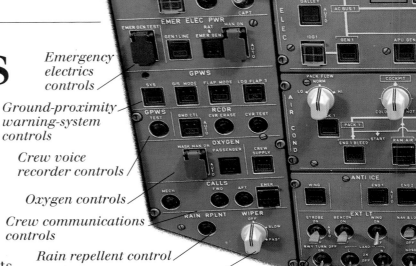

Emergency electrics controls

Ground-proximity warning-system controls

Crew voice recorder controls

Oxygen controls

Crew communications controls

Rain repellent control

Windshield wiper

External light controls

OVERHEAD PANEL

Navigation display mode selector

Mach (airspeed) selector

Navigation display in plan mode

Barometric control

Primary flight display

Screen transfer switch

**FLIGHT DECK SIMULATOR OF
AN AIRBUS A320 JETLINER**

Primary flight display brightness control

Loudspeaker control

Air vent

Loudspeaker

Footrest

Standby airspeed indicator

Standby altimeter

Standby artificial horizon

Rudder pedal adjuster

Digital distance and radio magnetic indicator (DDRMI)

Rudder pedal adjustment indicator

Systems data display

Display management panel

CAPTAIN'S SIDE

Footrest

Power lever

Audio control panel

Main panel floodlight control

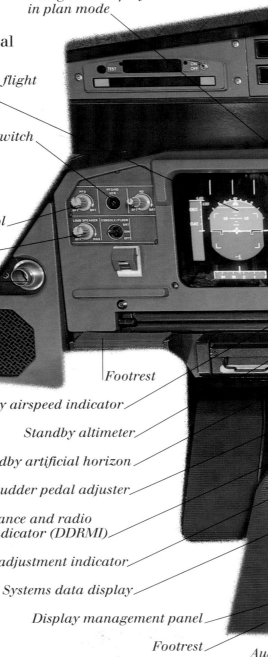

Flight computer controls

Cargo ventilation controls

Electrical controls

Cargo smoke controls

Avionic-ventilation controls

Air conditioning controls

Engine manual-start switches

Pressurization controls

Internal lights controls

Signs and emergency lights controls

Altitude preselect

Vertical-speed or flight-path angle selector

Navigation display range selector

Chronometer start/stop button

Altimeter

Tachometer

Navigation and communications radio controls

Artificial horizon

Airspeed indicator

Fuel gauge

Turn-and-slip indicator

Directional gyroscope

Vertical speed indicator

Voltmeter

Transponder

Water temperature gauge

COCKPIT PANEL OF AN ARV SUPER 2 MODERN LIGHT AIRCRAFT

Master warning light

Coaming panel

Master caution light

Navigation display in arc mode

Primary flight display

Chart- or map-holder

Air vent

Loudspeaker

Stowed table

Landing-gear indicator and automatic brake selector panel

Engine and warnings data display

Copilot's right rudder pedal

Brake-pressure indicator

Landing gear control handle

Chronometer

Flight-management and guidance-system control and display unit

Radio management panel

Table handle

Tail plane trimwheel

COPILOT'S SIDE

39

Supersonic jetliners

SUPERSONIC AIRCRAFT FLY FASTER than the speed of sound (Mach 1). There are many supersonic military aircraft, but only two supersonic passenger-carrying aircraft (also called SSTs, or supersonic transports) have been produced: the Russian Tu-144, and the Concorde, produced jointly by Britain and France. The Tu-144 had a greater maximum speed than the Concorde but was withdrawn in 1978, after only seven months in service. The Concorde has remained in service since 1976. It features many innovations, including a droop nose, which is lowered during takeoff and landing to aid visibility from the cockpit, and the pumping of fuel between forward and aft trim tanks to help stabilize the aircraft. The Concorde has a narrow fuselage and short-span wings to reduce drag during supersonic flight. Its noisy turbojet engines with afterburners enable it to carry 100 passengers at a cruising speed of Mach 2 at 50,000-60,000 ft (15,000-18,000 m). Once an aircraft is flying faster than Mach 1, it produces a continuous air-pressure wave, which is heard as a "sonic boom."

COMPUTER-DESIGNED SST

Strake · Fin · Standby pitot head · Inboard elevon-actuator fairing · Nose gear leg · Starboard outboard engine air intake

FRONT VIEW OF CONCORDE

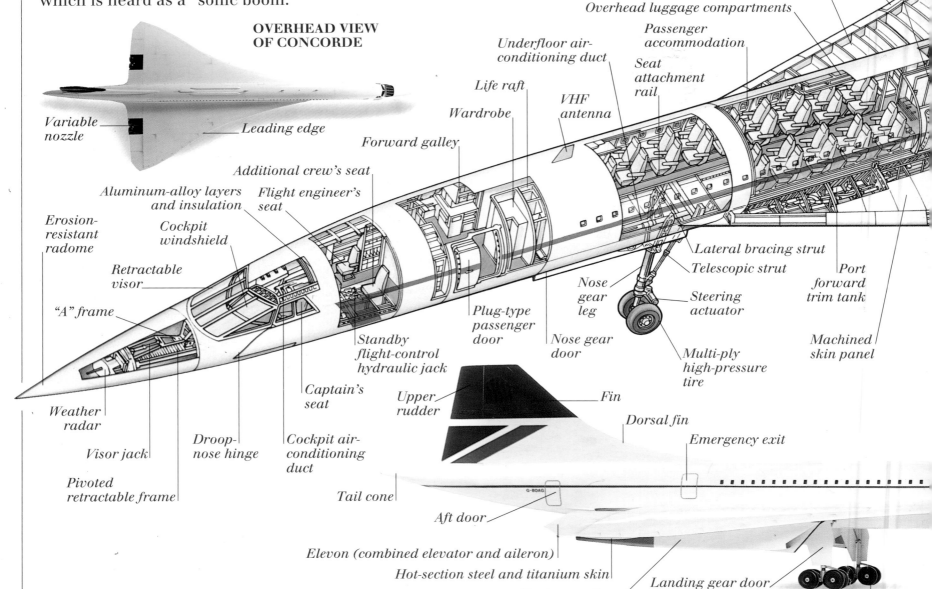

OVERHEAD VIEW OF CONCORDE

Variable nozzle · Leading edge

Toilets · Electrothermal deicing panel · Starboard forward trim tank · Overhead luggage compartments · Passenger accommodation · Seat attachment rail · Underfloor air-conditioning duct · Life raft · VHF antenna · Wardrobe · Forward galley · Additional crew's seat · Aluminum-alloy layers and insulation · Flight engineer's seat · Erosion-resistant radome · Cockpit windshield · Retractable visor · "A" frame · Weather radar · Visor jack · Pivoted retractable frame · Droop-nose hinge · Cockpit air-conditioning duct · Captain's seat · Standby flight-control hydraulic jack · Upper rudder · Plug-type passenger door · Nose gear door · Nose gear leg · Steering actuator · Telescopic strut · Lateral bracing strut · Multi-ply high-pressure tire · Port forward trim tank · Machined skin panel · Fin · Dorsal fin · Emergency exit · Tail cone · Aft door · Elevon (combined elevator and aileron) · Hot-section steel and titanium skin · Engine cowling · Landing gear door · Bogie main landing gear

40

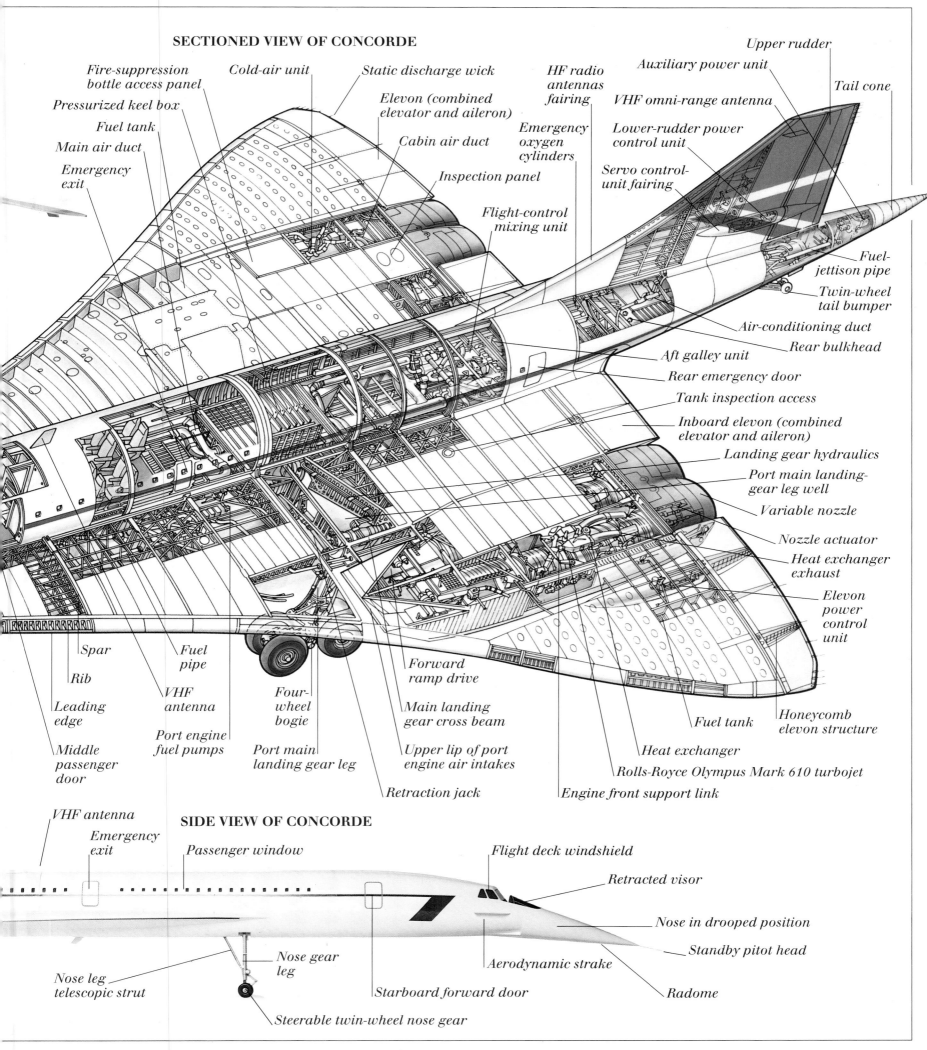

SECTIONED VIEW OF CONCORDE

Fire-suppression bottle access panel
Cold-air unit
Static discharge wick
Elevon (combined elevator and aileron)
HF radio antennas fairing
Upper rudder
Auxiliary power unit
Tail cone
VHF omni-range antenna
Pressurized keel box
Fuel tank
Cabin air duct
Emergency oxygen cylinders
Lower-rudder power control unit
Main air duct
Inspection panel
Servo control-unit fairing
Emergency exit
Flight-control mixing unit
Fuel-jettison pipe
Twin-wheel tail bumper
Air-conditioning duct
Rear bulkhead
Aft galley unit
Rear emergency door
Tank inspection access
Inboard elevon (combined elevator and aileron)
Landing gear hydraulics
Port main landing-gear leg well
Variable nozzle
Nozzle actuator
Heat exchanger exhaust
Elevon power control unit
Spar
Fuel pipe
Forward ramp drive
Rib
VHF antenna
Four-wheel bogie
Main landing gear cross beam
Fuel tank
Honeycomb elevon structure
Leading edge
Heat exchanger
Middle passenger door
Port engine fuel pumps
Port main landing gear leg
Upper lip of port engine air intakes
Rolls-Royce Olympus Mark 610 turbojet
Retraction jack
Engine front support link

SIDE VIEW OF CONCORDE

VHF antenna
Emergency exit
Passenger window
Flight deck windshield
Retracted visor
Nose in drooped position
Standby pitot head
Nose gear leg
Aerodynamic strake
Nose leg telescopic strut
Starboard forward door
Radome
Steerable twin-wheel nose gear

Jet engines

JET ENGINES ARE USED BY MOST MILITARY and heavy aircraft and by many helicopters. The simplest type of jet engine, or gas turbine, is the turbojet. It works by continuously burning a mixture of fuel and air in a combustion chamber to produce a jet of hot exhaust gas that is expelled through a nozzle to produce thrust. The hot gas also spins turbine blades which, in turn, spin the blades of an air compressor; the compressor forces air into the combustion chamber. Many of the fastest aircraft use turbojets, with additional booster units called afterburners, but their use is restricted by their high noise emission. Most jetliners use quieter turbofan jet engines. An enormous fan, driven by a low-pressure turbine, feeds some air into the compressor but feeds most of it through bypass ducts to join the exhaust jetstream in the tail cone. The bypass stream produces most of the thrust. Many smaller, propeller-driven aircraft use turboprop jet engines, in which the engine powers a propeller.

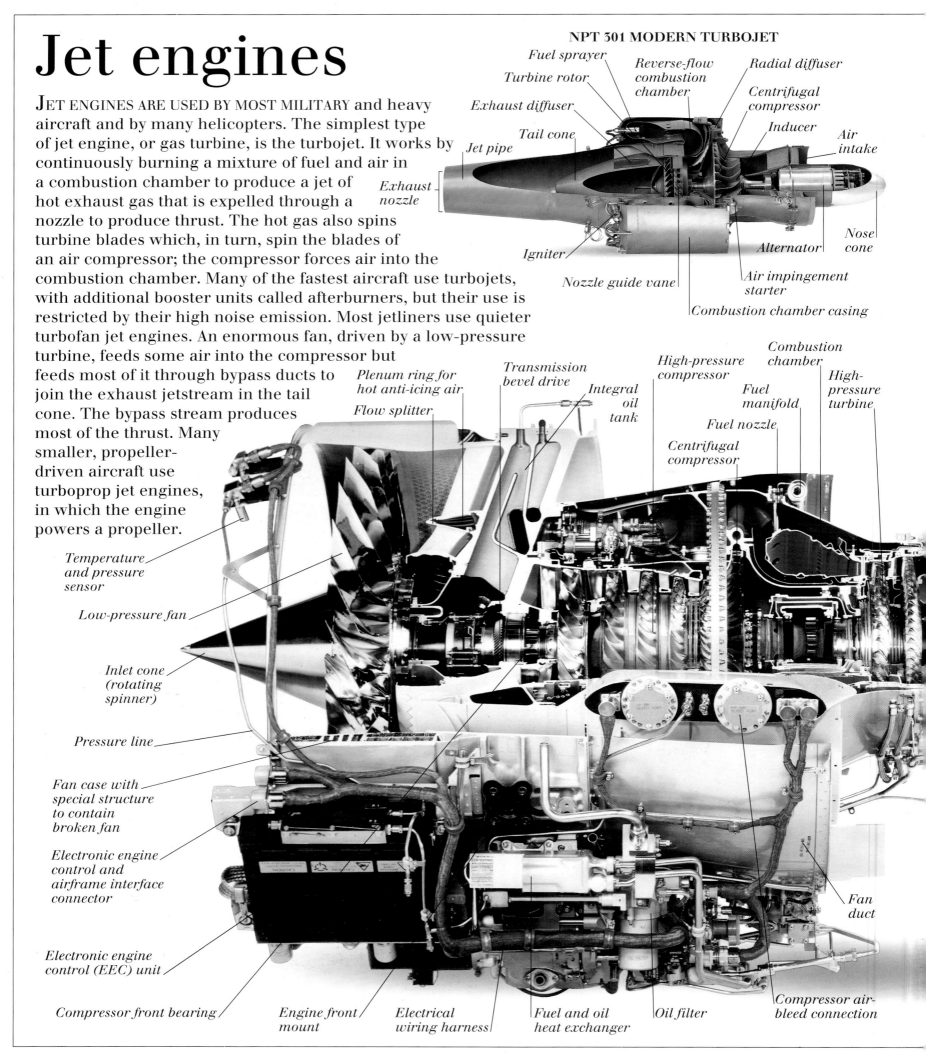

NPT 301 MODERN TURBOJET

Fuel sprayer
Turbine rotor
Reverse-flow combustion chamber
Radial diffuser
Centrifugal compressor
Exhaust diffuser
Inducer
Tail cone
Air intake
Jet pipe
Exhaust nozzle
Igniter
Nozzle guide vane
Air impingement starter
Combustion chamber casing
Alternator
Nose cone

Plenum ring for hot anti-icing air
Transmission bevel drive
High-pressure compressor
Combustion chamber
High-pressure turbine
Flow splitter
Integral oil tank
Fuel manifold
Centrifugal compressor
Fuel nozzle
Temperature and pressure sensor
Low-pressure fan
Inlet cone (rotating spinner)
Pressure line
Fan case with special structure to contain broken fan
Electronic engine control and airframe interface connector
Electronic engine control (EEC) unit
Compressor front bearing
Engine front mount
Electrical wiring harness
Fuel and oil heat exchanger
Oil filter
Compressor air-bleed connection
Fan duct

42

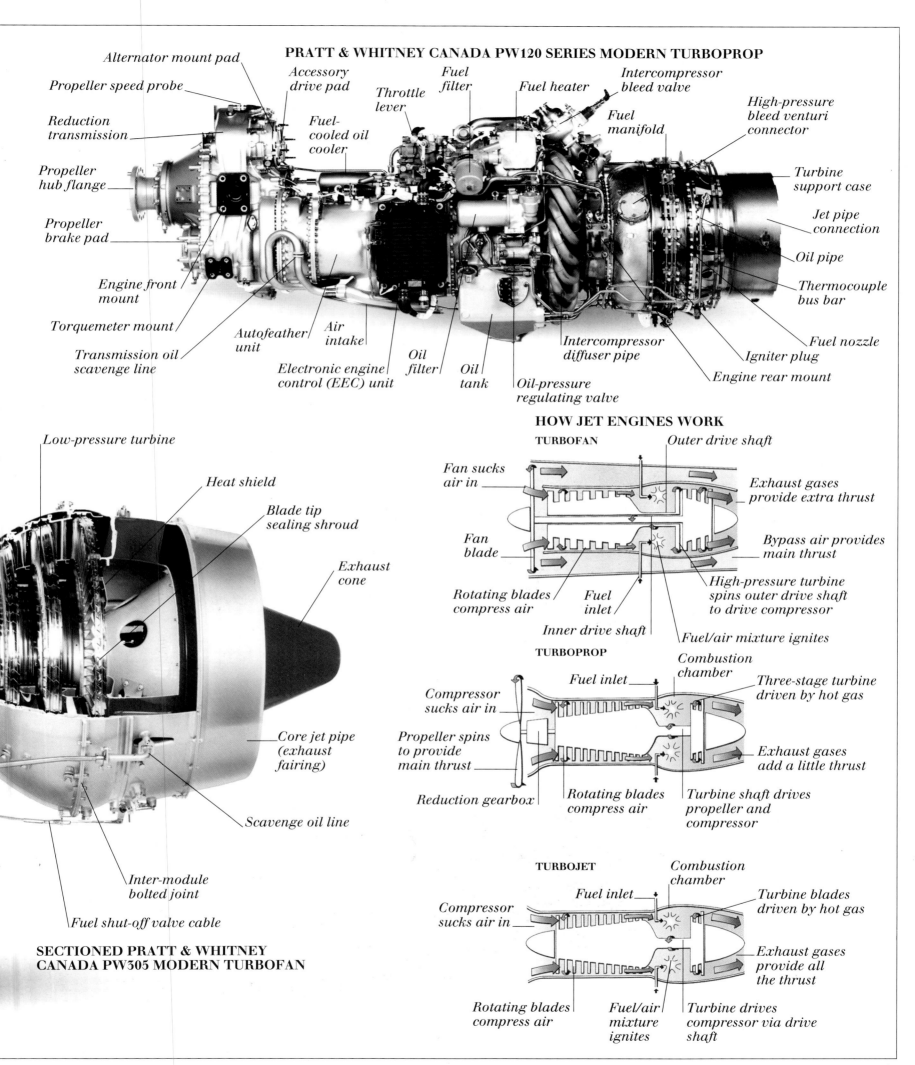

PRATT & WHITNEY CANADA PW120 SERIES MODERN TURBOPROP

Alternator mount pad
Propeller speed probe
Reduction transmission
Accessory drive pad
Throttle lever
Fuel filter
Fuel heater
Intercompressor bleed valve
Fuel manifold
High-pressure bleed venturi connector
Propeller hub flange
Fuel-cooled oil cooler
Turbine support case
Jet pipe connection
Propeller brake pad
Oil pipe
Engine front mount
Thermocouple bus bar
Torquemeter mount
Autofeather unit
Air intake
Oil filter
Oil tank
Intercompressor diffuser pipe
Fuel nozzle
Igniter plug
Engine rear mount
Transmission oil scavenge line
Electronic engine control (EEC) unit
Oil-pressure regulating valve

SECTIONED PRATT & WHITNEY CANADA PW305 MODERN TURBOFAN

Low-pressure turbine
Heat shield
Blade tip sealing shroud
Exhaust cone
Core jet pipe (exhaust fairing)
Scavenge oil line
Inter-module bolted joint
Fuel shut-off valve cable

HOW JET ENGINES WORK

TURBOFAN

Fan sucks air in
Outer drive shaft
Exhaust gases provide extra thrust
Fan blade
Bypass air provides main thrust
Rotating blades compress air
Fuel inlet
High-pressure turbine spins outer drive shaft to drive compressor
Inner drive shaft
Fuel/air mixture ignites

TURBOPROP

Fuel inlet
Combustion chamber
Compressor sucks air in
Three-stage turbine driven by hot gas
Propeller spins to provide main thrust
Exhaust gases add a little thrust
Reduction gearbox
Rotating blades compress air
Turbine shaft drives propeller and compressor

TURBOJET

Fuel inlet
Combustion chamber
Compressor sucks air in
Turbine blades driven by hot gas
Exhaust gases provide all the thrust
Rotating blades compress air
Fuel/air mixture ignites
Turbine drives compressor via drive shaft

Modern military aircraft

MODERN MILITARY AIRCRAFT ARE AMONG THE MOST SOPHISTICATED and expensive products of the 20th century. Fighters need computer-operated controls for maneuverability, powerful engines, and effective air-to-air weapons. Most modern fighters also have guided missiles, radar, and passive, infrared sensors. These developments enable today's fighters to engage in combat with adversaries who are outside visual range. Bombers carry a large weapon load and enough fuel for long-range flights. A few military aircraft, such as the Tornado and the F-14 Tomcat, have variable-sweep ("swing") wings. During takeoff and landing their wings are fully extended, but for high-speed flight and low-level attacks the wings are pivoted fully back. A recent development is the "stealth" bomber, which is designed to absorb or deflect enemy radar in order to remain undetected. Earlier bombers, such as the Tornado, use terrain-following radars to fly so close to the ground that they avoid enemy radar detection.

FRONT VIEW OF A PANAVIA TORNADO

Instrument landing system antenna

Birdproof windshield

Air data probe

Port variable-incidence air intake

Wing-root glove fairing

Starboard inboard stores pylon

Taileron

Starboard main landing-gear door

Main landing-gear leg

Laser ranger and marked-target seeker

Starboard nose gear door

Steerable twin-wheel nose gear

Radome containing ground-mapping, attack, and terrain-following radars

Taxiing light

Wing extended for takeoff and landing

Wing pivoted back for high-speed flight

SWING-WING F-14 TOMCAT FIGHTER

SIDE VIEW OF A PANAVIA TORNADO GR1A (RECONNAISSANCE VERSION), 1986

Pilot's cockpit

Navigator's instrument console

Navigator's cockpit

Single canopy over both cockpits

Engine air intake

Navigation light

Flat, birdproof windshield

High-velocity air duct to disperse rain

Upper "request identification" antenna

Air data probe

Radome containing ground-mapping, attack, and terrain-following radars

UHF antenna

Angle-of-attack probe

Tacan (tactical air navigation) antenna

Emergency canopy release handle

Nose gear door

Steerable nose gear leg

Pitot head

Twin nose-wheel

Window covering infrared reconnaissance camera

Hinged auxiliary air intake

Cold-air intake (ram scoop)

Heat exchanger exhaust duct

RESCUE

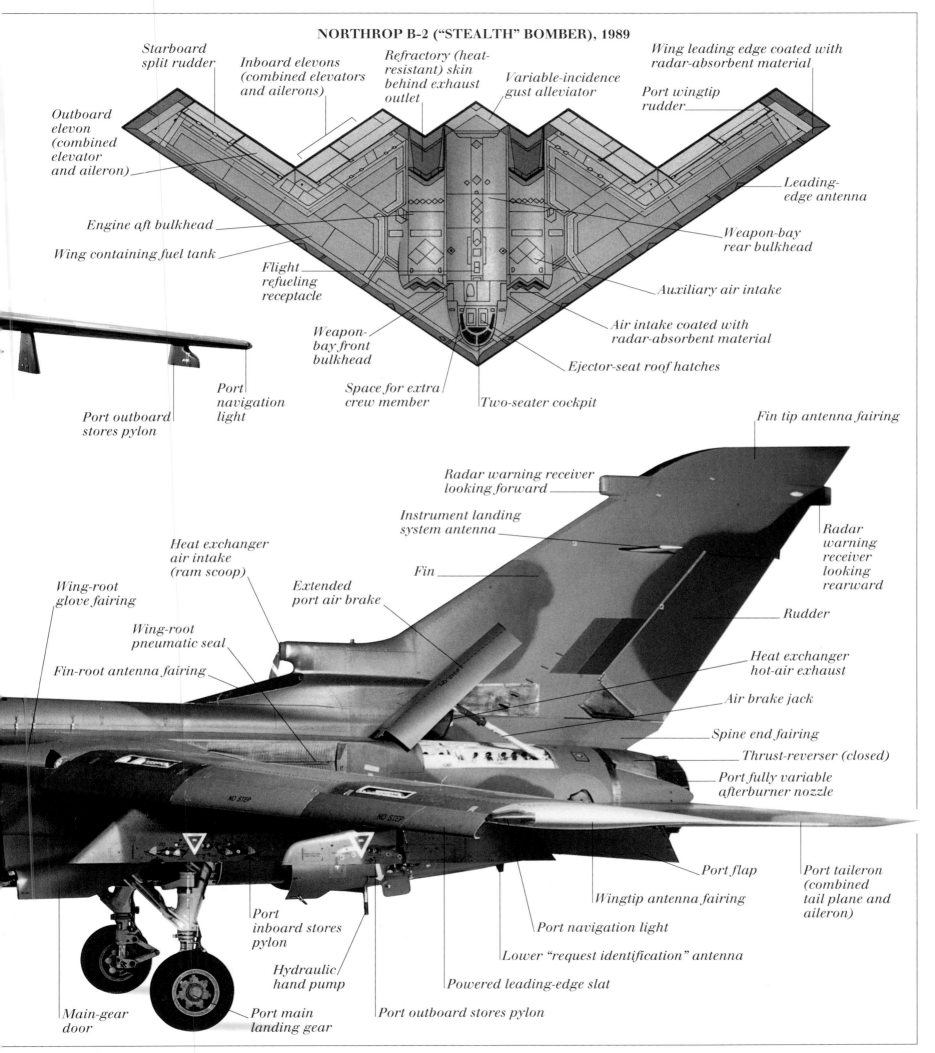

NORTHROP B-2 ("STEALTH" BOMBER), 1989

Starboard split rudder

Inboard elevons (combined elevators and ailerons)

Refractory (heat-resistant) skin behind exhaust outlet

Variable-incidence gust alleviator

Wing leading edge coated with radar-absorbent material

Port wingtip rudder

Outboard elevon (combined elevator and aileron)

Leading-edge antenna

Engine aft bulkhead

Wing containing fuel tank

Weapon-bay rear bulkhead

Flight refueling receptacle

Auxiliary air intake

Weapon-bay front bulkhead

Air intake coated with radar-absorbent material

Port navigation light

Port outboard stores pylon

Space for extra crew member

Ejector-seat roof hatches

Two-seater cockpit

Fin tip antenna fairing

Radar warning receiver looking forward

Instrument landing system antenna

Radar warning receiver looking rearward

Fin

Heat exchanger air intake (ram scoop)

Extended port air brake

Rudder

Wing-root glove fairing

Wing-root pneumatic seal

Heat exchanger hot-air exhaust

Air brake jack

Fin-root antenna fairing

Spine end fairing

Thrust-reverser (closed)

Port fully variable afterburner nozzle

Port inboard stores pylon

Port flap

Port taileron (combined tail plane and aileron)

Hydraulic hand pump

Wingtip antenna fairing

Main-gear door

Port main landing gear

Port navigation light

Lower "request identification" antenna

Port outboard stores pylon

Powered leading-edge slat

45

Helicopters

HELICOPTERS USE ROTATING BLADES for lift, propulsion, and steering. The first machine to achieve sustained, controlled flight using rotating blades was the autogiro built in the 1920s by Juan de la Cierva of Spain. His machine had unpowered blades above the fuselage that relied on the flow of air to rotate them and provide lift while the autogiro was driven forward by a conventional propeller. Then, in 1939, the Russian-born American Igor Sikorsky produced his VS-300, the forerunner of the modern helicopter. Its engine-driven blades provided lift, propulsion, and steering. It could take off vertically, hover, and fly in any direction, and had a tail rotor to prevent the helicopter body from spinning (see pp. 48-49). The introduction of gas turbine jet engines to helicopters in 1955 produced quieter, safer, and more powerful machines. Because of their versatility in flight, helicopters are used today for many purposes, including crop spraying, traffic surveillance, and transporting crews to deep-sea oil rigs, as well as acting as gunships, air ambulances, and air taxis.

BELL 47G-3B1

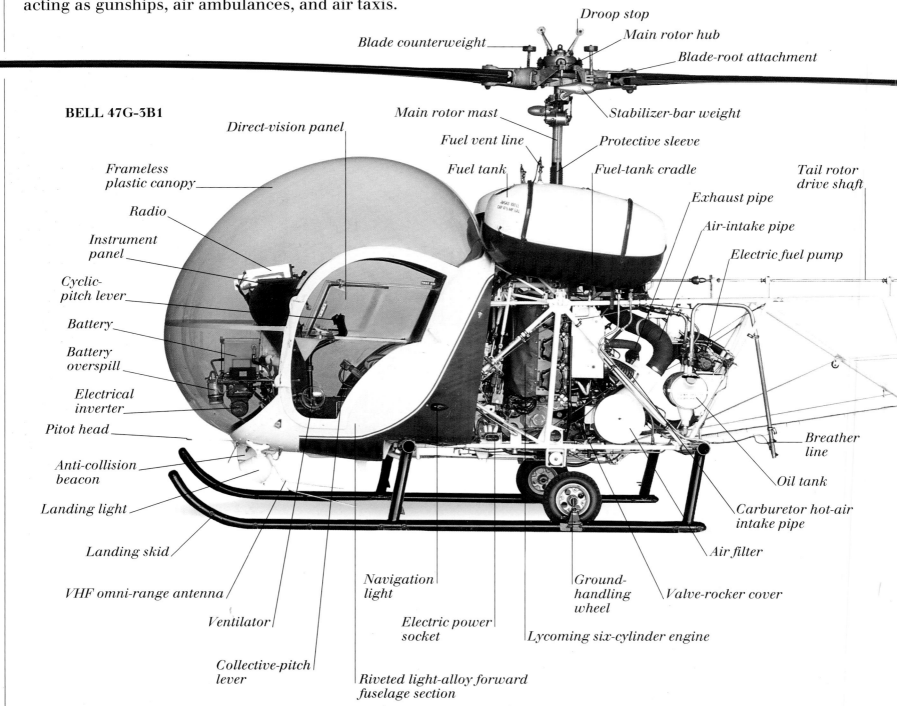

BELL 47G-3B1

Droop stop
Blade counterweight
Main rotor hub
Blade-root attachment
Main rotor mast
Stabilizer-bar weight
Direct-vision panel
Fuel vent line
Protective sleeve
Fuel tank
Fuel-tank cradle
Frameless plastic canopy
Tail rotor drive shaft
Exhaust pipe
Radio
Air-intake pipe
Instrument panel
Electric fuel pump
Cyclic-pitch lever
Battery
Battery overspill
Electrical inverter
Pitot head
Breather line
Anti-collision beacon
Oil tank
Landing light
Carburetor hot-air intake pipe
Landing skid
Air filter
VHF omni-range antenna
Navigation light
Ground-handling wheel
Valve-rocker cover
Ventilator
Electric power socket
Lycoming six-cylinder engine
Collective-pitch lever
Riveted light-alloy forward fuselage section

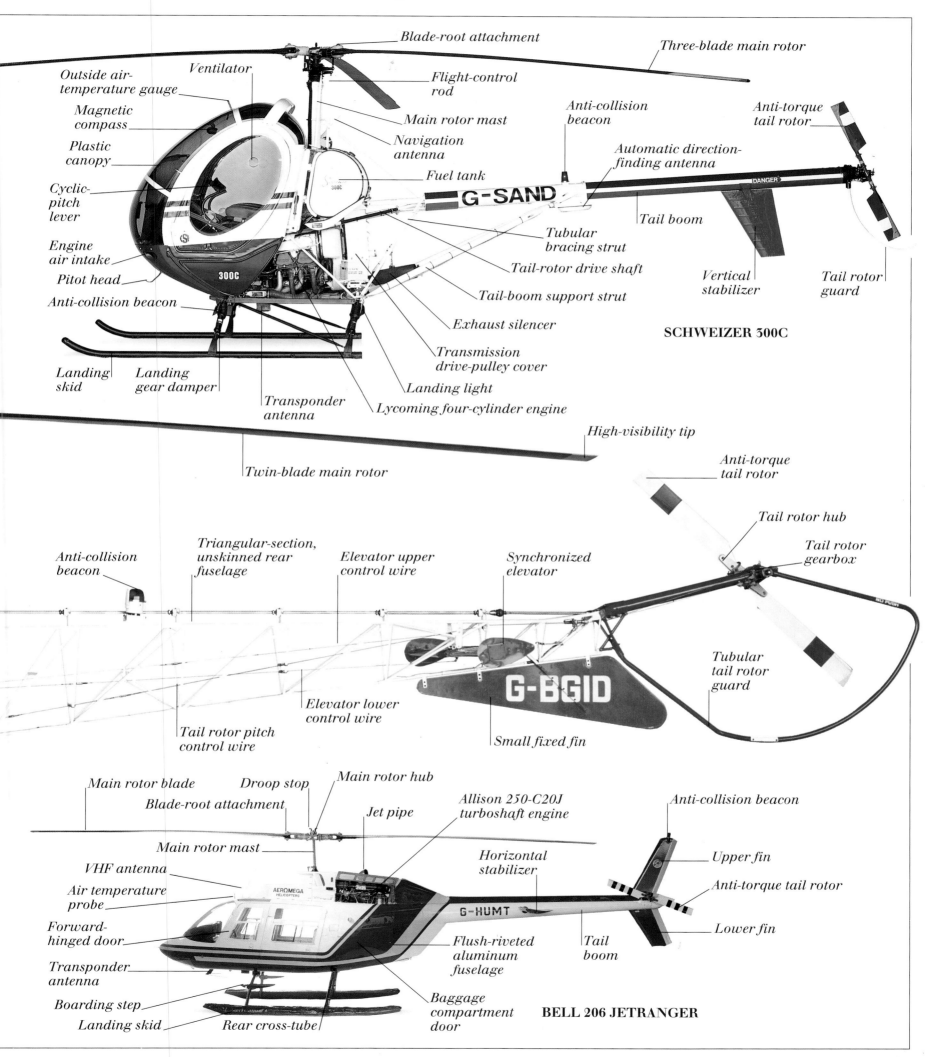

Blade-root attachment

Three-blade main rotor

Ventilator

Flight-control rod

Outside air-temperature gauge

Anti-collision beacon

Anti-torque tail rotor

Magnetic compass

Main rotor mast

Automatic direction-finding antenna

Navigation antenna

Plastic canopy

Cyclic-pitch lever

Fuel tank

G-SAND

Tail boom

Engine air intake

Tubular bracing strut

Pitot head

Tail-rotor drive shaft

Vertical stabilizer

Tail rotor guard

Anti-collision beacon

Tail-boom support strut

Exhaust silencer

SCHWEIZER 300C

Landing skid

Landing gear damper

Transmission drive-pulley cover

Transponder antenna

Landing light

Lycoming four-cylinder engine

High-visibility tip

Twin-blade main rotor

Anti-torque tail rotor

Triangular-section, unskinned rear fuselage

Elevator upper control wire

Synchronized elevator

Tail rotor hub

Anti-collision beacon

Tail rotor gearbox

G-BGID

Tubular tail rotor guard

Elevator lower control wire

Tail rotor pitch control wire

Small fixed fin

Main rotor blade

Droop stop

Main rotor hub

Allison 250-C20J turboshaft engine

Anti-collision beacon

Blade-root attachment

Jet pipe

Main rotor mast

Horizontal stabilizer

Upper fin

VHF antenna

Anti-torque tail rotor

Air temperature probe

AEROMEGA HELICOPTERS

G-HUMT

Lower fin

Forward-hinged door

Flush-riveted aluminum fuselage

Tail boom

Transponder antenna

Boarding step

Baggage compartment door

BELL 206 JETRANGER

Landing skid

Rear cross-tube

47

Helicopter technology

HELICOPTERS CAN FLY in any direction, or simply hover in one place. This versatility is made possible by a complex system of controls that allows the pilot to alter the angle of the blades on the main rotor and the tail rotor. The tail rotor maintains a sideways thrust to counteract the tendency of the helicopter to spin in the opposite direction to the main rotor; the pitch (angle) of the tail rotor blades is altered by the anti-torque pedals to swing the tail left or right. To fly up or down, the pitch of the main rotor blades is adjusted using the collective-pitch lever. To fly forward, the entire main rotor is tilted forward using the cyclic-pitch lever; the same lever tilts the rotor to fly backward or to the side. Both levers perform their operations via the swash plates, which are connected to the main rotor blades by push-pull rods. To hover, the pilot must maintain a precise balance between both levers and the anti-torque pedals. The complex movements of the rotor blades are made possible by the main rotor hub. On two-bladed rotors, the blades are bolted directly on to the hub, but on rotors with more than two blades, the blades are attached to hinges on the hub to allow the blades to flap slightly when rotating.

MAIN ROTOR HUB

Drag brace · Mast attachment point · Drive splines · Blade bolt · Blade-root attachment · Hub · Counterweight · Pitch-change horn · Jesus thread · Hub drive splines · Stabilizer-bar drive splines · Damper drive splines · Main rotor mast · Swash plate drive splines · Hydraulic reservoir · Transmission drive splines

Hydraulic pump · Filter · Relief valve

MECHANICAL COMPONENTS OF A BELL 47 G-SERIES

Link from copilot's cyclic-pitch lever to jackshaft · Jackshaft · Servo-jack pilot valve · Servo-jack ram · Elevator link · Elevator jackshaft · Fore-and-aft servo-jack body · Link to fore-and-aft servo-jack · Link from pilot's cyclic-pitch lever to jackshaft · Link from jackshaft to fore-and-aft servo-jack · Hydraulic valve · Servo-jack support · Link from servo-jack ram to fore-and-aft pitch horn

DUAL FORE-AND-AFT CYCLIC CONTROLS

Copilot's tail rotor pedal (anti-torque pedal) · Pedal to jackshaft link · Jackshaft · Quadrant · Bellcrank · Pilot's tail rotor pedal (anti-torque pedal) · Tail rotor cable

Link from copilot's cyclic-pitch lever to bellcrank · Copilot's cyclic-pitch lever · Copilot's collective-pitch lever · Link to throttle · Jackshaft · Cam box · Link to throttle cam · Throttle shaft · Servo-jack support · Airframe mount · Link to servo-jack · Link to bellcrank · Bellcrank · Collective jackshaft · Lateral servo-jack · Torque shaft · Link to servo-jack · Link from torque shaft to lateral-pitch horn · Pilot's cyclic-pitch lever · Electric cable · Throttle twist-grip · Starter button · Pilot's collective-pitch lever

TAIL ROTOR CONTROLS   **DUAL COLLECTIVE AND LATERAL CYCLIC CONTROLS, AND THROTTLE LINKAGE**

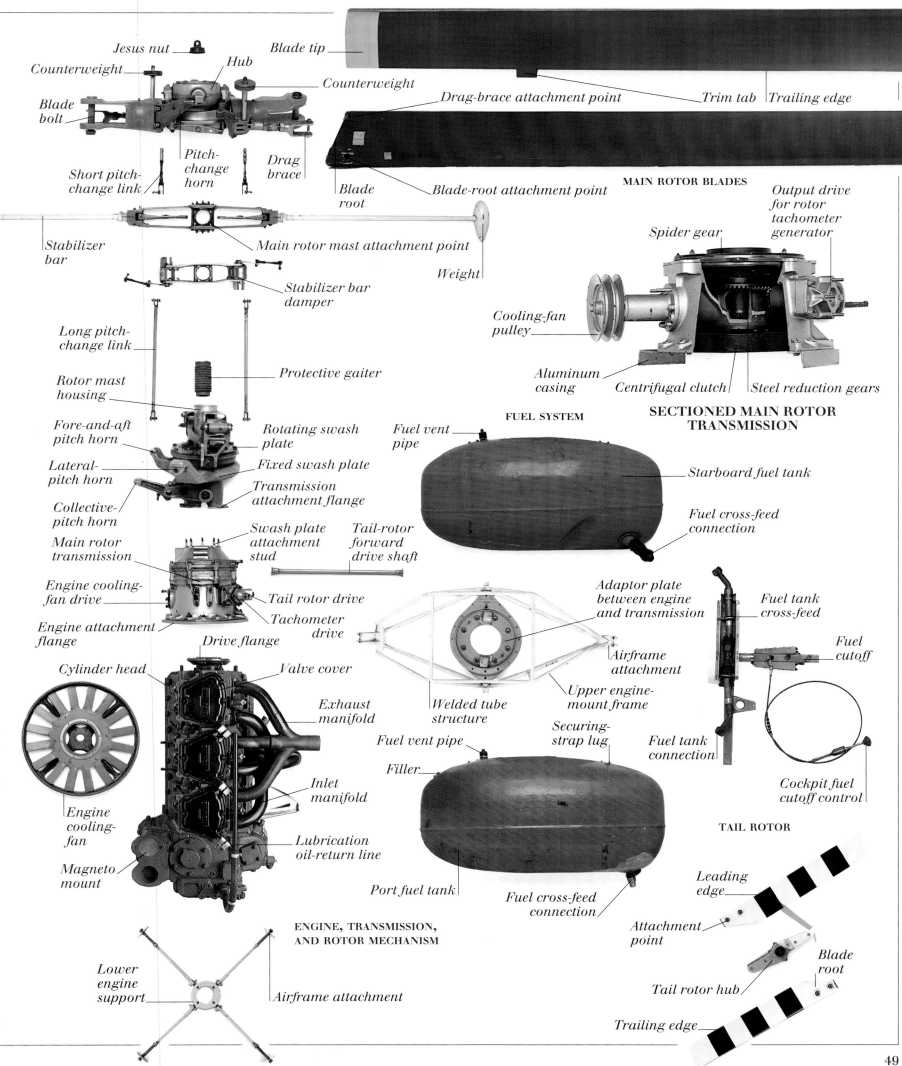

Jesus nut

Counterweight

Hub

Blade tip

Counterweight

Blade bolt

Pitch-change horn

Drag brace

Drag-brace attachment point

Trim tab

Trailing edge

Short pitch-change link

Blade root

Blade-root attachment point

MAIN ROTOR BLADES

Stabilizer bar

Main rotor mast attachment point

Weight

Output drive for rotor tachometer generator

Spider gear

Stabilizer bar damper

Cooling-fan pulley

Long pitch-change link

Rotor mast housing

Protective gaiter

Aluminum casing

Centrifugal clutch

Steel reduction gears

Fore-and-aft pitch horn

Rotating swash plate

SECTIONED MAIN ROTOR TRANSMISSION

Lateral-pitch horn

Fixed swash plate

FUEL SYSTEM

Fuel vent pipe

Collective-pitch horn

Transmission attachment flange

Main rotor transmission

Swash plate attachment stud

Tail-rotor forward drive shaft

Starboard fuel tank

Fuel cross-feed connection

Engine cooling-fan drive

Tail rotor drive

Adaptor plate between engine and transmission

Fuel tank cross-feed

Engine attachment flange

Tachometer drive

Airframe attachment

Fuel cutoff

Cylinder head

Drive flange

Valve cover

Upper engine-mount frame

Fuel tank connection

Exhaust manifold

Welded tube structure

Securing-strap lug

Fuel vent pipe

Inlet manifold

Filler

Cockpit fuel cutoff control

Engine cooling-fan

Lubrication oil-return line

TAIL ROTOR

Magneto mount

Port fuel tank

Fuel cross-feed connection

Leading edge

ENGINE, TRANSMISSION, AND ROTOR MECHANISM

Attachment point

Lower engine support

Airframe attachment

Blade root

Tail rotor hub

Trailing edge

Light aircraft

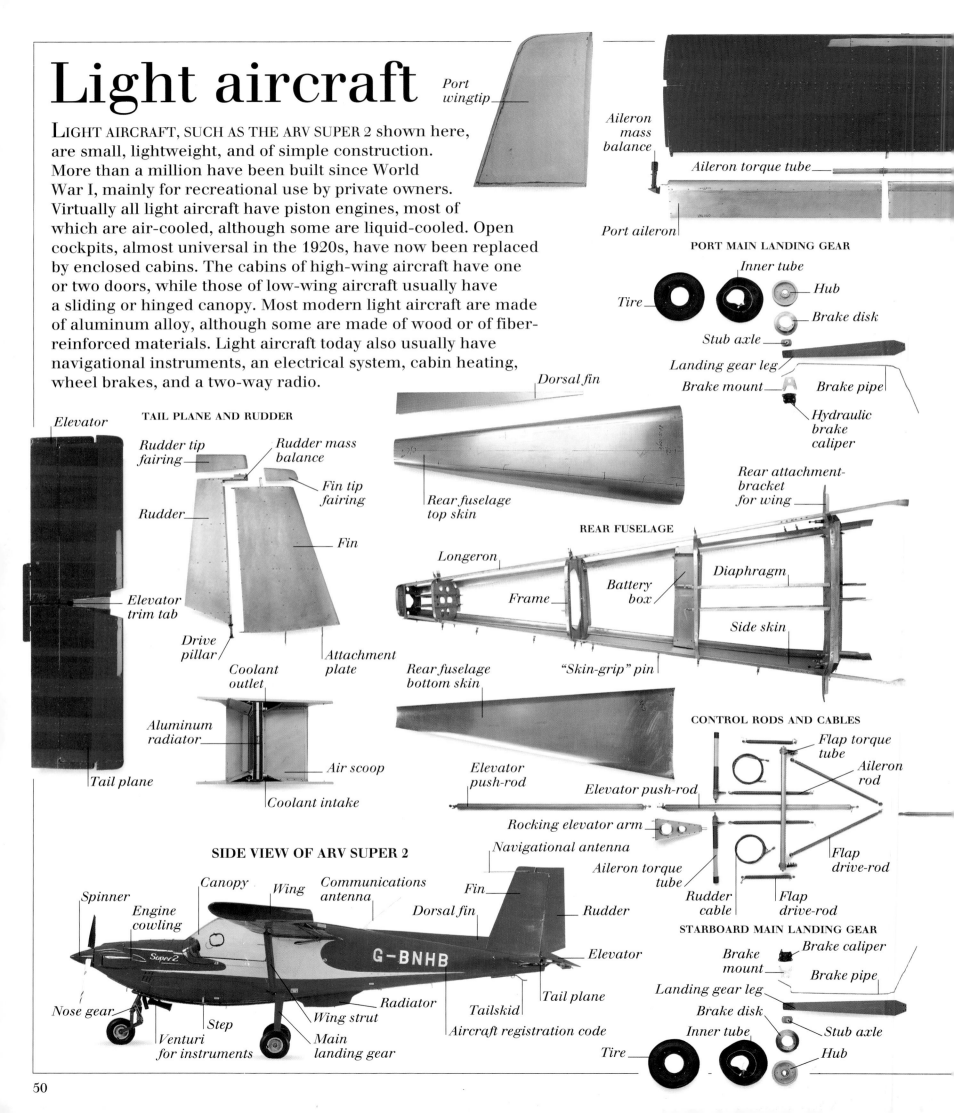

LIGHT AIRCRAFT, SUCH AS THE ARV SUPER 2 shown here, are small, lightweight, and of simple construction. More than a million have been built since World War I, mainly for recreational use by private owners. Virtually all light aircraft have piston engines, most of which are air-cooled, although some are liquid-cooled. Open cockpits, almost universal in the 1920s, have now been replaced by enclosed cabins. The cabins of high-wing aircraft have one or two doors, while those of low-wing aircraft usually have a sliding or hinged canopy. Most modern light aircraft are made of aluminum alloy, although some are made of wood or of fiber-reinforced materials. Light aircraft today also usually have navigational instruments, an electrical system, cabin heating, wheel brakes, and a two-way radio.

Port wingtip

Aileron mass balance

Aileron torque tube

Port aileron

PORT MAIN LANDING GEAR

Inner tube

Hub

Tire

Brake disk

Stub axle

Landing gear leg

Brake mount

Brake pipe

Hydraulic brake caliper

Elevator

TAIL PLANE AND RUDDER

Rudder tip fairing

Rudder mass balance

Fin tip fairing

Rudder

Fin

Dorsal fin

Rear fuselage top skin

Elevator trim tab

Drive pillar

Coolant outlet

Attachment plate

Rear attachment-bracket for wing

REAR FUSELAGE

Longeron

Diaphragm

Frame

Battery box

Aluminum radiator

Side skin

Tail plane

Rear fuselage bottom skin

"Skin-grip" pin

Air scoop

Coolant intake

CONTROL RODS AND CABLES

Flap torque tube

Elevator push-rod

Aileron rod

Elevator push-rod

Rocking elevator arm

Navigational antenna

Aileron torque tube

Flap drive-rod

SIDE VIEW OF ARV SUPER 2

Canopy

Wing

Communications antenna

Fin

Dorsal fin

Rudder

Spinner

Engine cowling

Rudder cable

Flap drive-rod

STARBOARD MAIN LANDING GEAR

Brake caliper

Brake mount

Brake pipe

Elevator

Nose gear

Step

Venturi for instruments

Radiator

Wing strut

Main landing gear

Tailskid

Tail plane

Aircraft registration code

Landing gear leg

Brake disk

Inner tube

Tire

Stub axle

Hub

G-BNHB

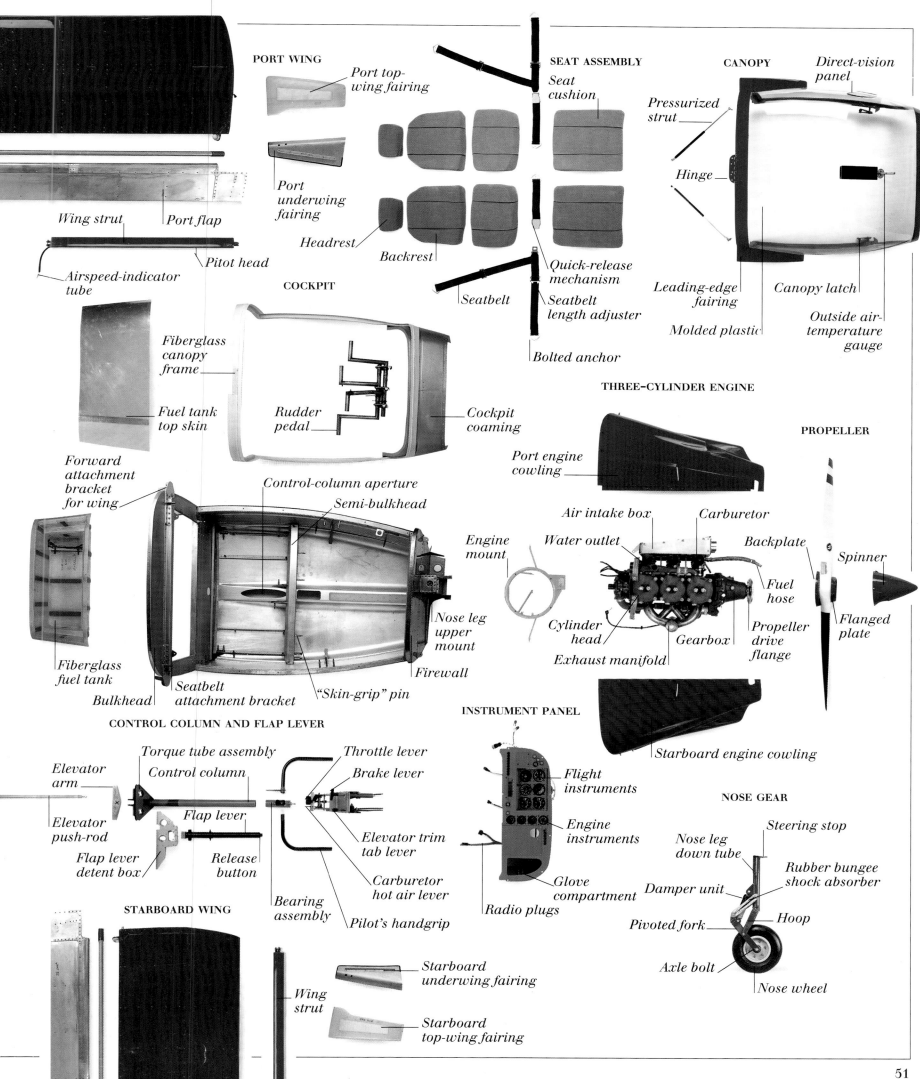

PORT WING

Port top-wing fairing

Port underwing fairing

Headrest

Wing strut

Port flap

Pitot head

Airspeed-indicator tube

SEAT ASSEMBLY

Seat cushion

Backrest

Seatbelt

Quick-release mechanism

Seatbelt length adjuster

Bolted anchor

COCKPIT

Fiberglass canopy frame

Fuel tank top skin

Rudder pedal

Cockpit coaming

CANOPY

Direct-vision panel

Pressurized strut

Hinge

Leading-edge fairing

Canopy latch

Molded plastic

Outside air-temperature gauge

THREE-CYLINDER ENGINE

Port engine cowling

Air intake box

Water outlet

Carburetor

Backplate

PROPELLER

Spinner

Flanged plate

Engine mount

Fuel hose

Cylinder head

Gearbox

Propeller drive flange

Exhaust manifold

Forward attachment bracket for wing

Control-column aperture

Semi-bulkhead

Nose leg upper mount

Fiberglass fuel tank

Firewall

Bulkhead

Seatbelt attachment bracket

"Skin-grip" pin

Starboard engine cowling

CONTROL COLUMN AND FLAP LEVER

Torque tube assembly

Control column

Elevator arm

Flap lever

Elevator push-rod

Flap lever detent box

Release button

Throttle lever

Brake lever

Elevator trim tab lever

Carburetor hot air lever

Bearing assembly

Pilot's handgrip

INSTRUMENT PANEL

Flight instruments

Engine instruments

Glove compartment

Radio plugs

NOSE GEAR

Steering stop

Nose leg down tube

Rubber bungee shock absorber

Damper unit

Hoop

Pivoted fork

Axle bolt

Nose wheel

STARBOARD WING

Wing strut

Starboard underwing fairing

Starboard top-wing fairing

Gliders, hang gliders, and ultralights

MODERN GLIDERS ARE AMONG the most graceful and aerodynamically efficient of all aircraft. Unpowered but with a large wingspan (up to about 82 ft, or 25 m), gliders use currents of hot, rising air (thermals) to stay aloft, and a rudder, elevators, and ailerons for control. Modern gliders have achieved flights of more than 900 miles (1,450 km) and altitudes above 49,000 ft (15,000 m). Hang gliders consist of a simple frame across which rigid or flexible material is stretched to form the wings. The pilot is suspended below the wings in a harness or body bag and, gripping a triangular A-frame, steers by shifting weight from side to side. Like gliders, hang gliders rely on thermals for lift. Ultralights are basically powered hang gliders. A small engine and an open fiberglass car (trike), which can hold a crew of two, are suspended beneath a stronger version of a hang glider frame; the frame may have rigid or flexible wings. Ultralight pilots, like hang glider pilots, steer by shifting their weight against an A-frame. Ultralights can reach speeds of up to 100 mph (160 kph).

HANG GLIDER

NOSE SHELL

Grommet for front pylon strut

Instrument panel

PEGASUS XL SE ULTRALIGHT

King post

Apex

Stiffening rib

Center-line beam

Main suspension

Rear-mounted propeller (pusher propeller)

Fuel tank

Wheel part

Main wheel

Trike nacelle

Apex wire

Nose shell

Fixed nose wheel

Nose gear mount

Trailing edge

End of rib

Dacron skin

HANG GLIDER BODY BAG

Clip-in latch for pilot

Shoulder strap

Layers of insulating fabric

Camera pouch

Armhole

Shoulder pad

Body bag

SCHLEICHER K23 GLIDER

Down turned wingtip acts as skid

Aileron

Aluminum air brake

Radio antenna

Tail plane

Hinged elevator

Single pilot cockpit

Forward-opening canopy

Towing hook

Nose wheel

Nonretractable main wheel

Fuselage of fiberglass and foam layers

T-type cantilevered fin

EVW

Rudder

Tailwheel

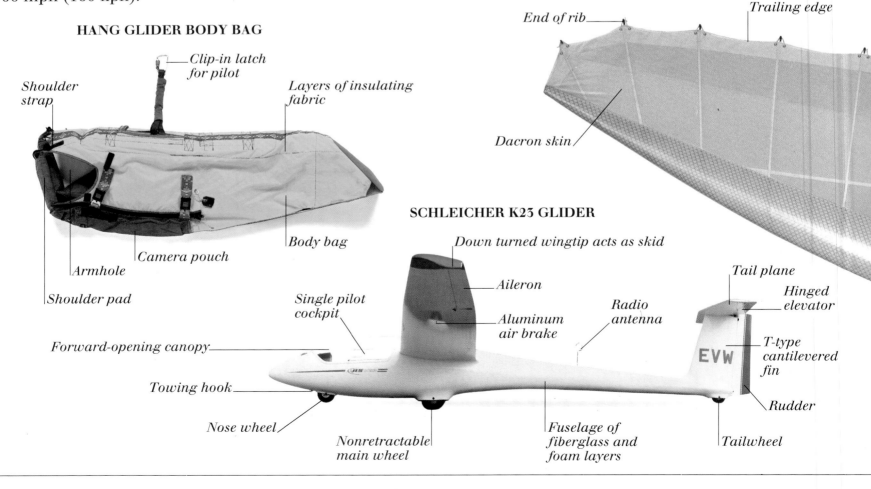

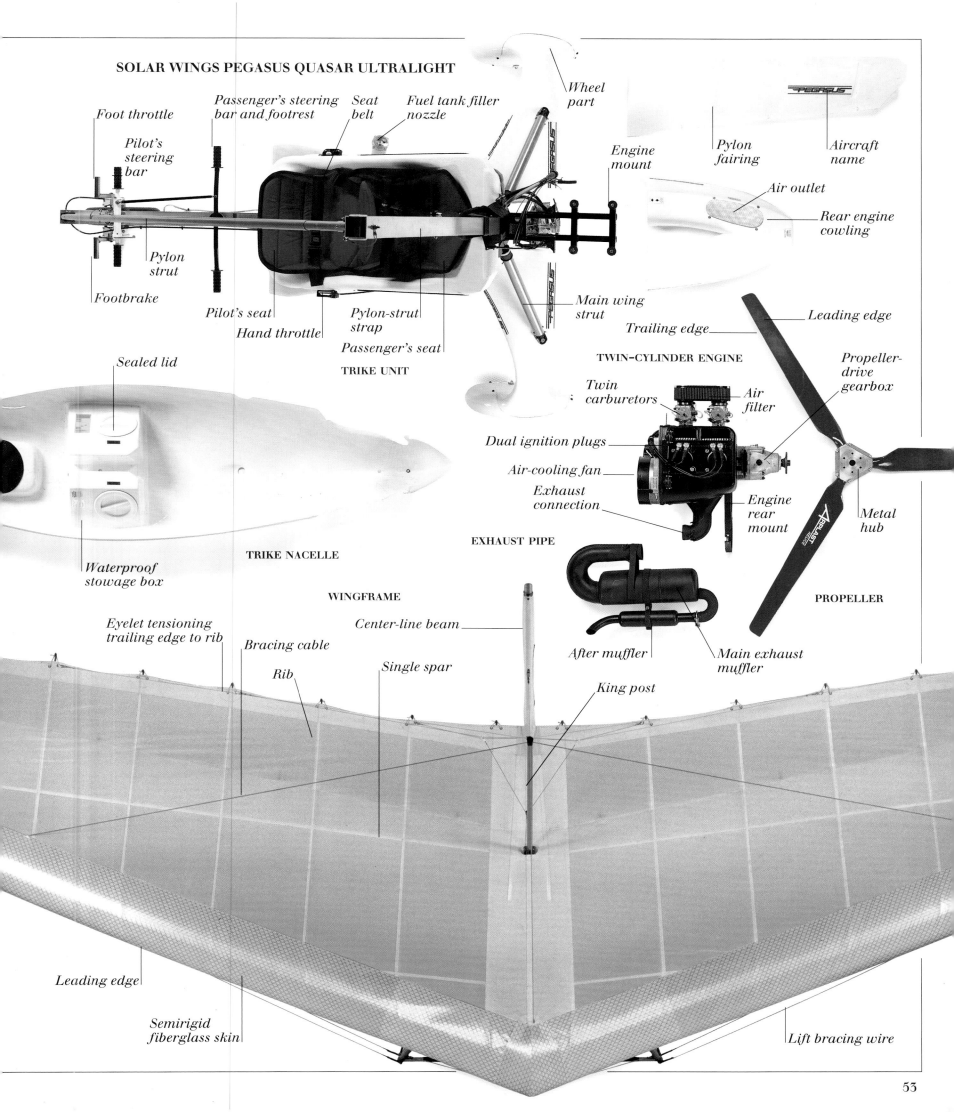

SOLAR WINGS PEGASUS QUASAR ULTRALIGHT

Foot throttle

Passenger's steering bar and footrest

Seat belt

Fuel tank filler nozzle

Wheel part

Pilot's steering bar

Engine mount

Pylon fairing

Aircraft name

Air outlet

Rear engine cowling

Pylon strut

Footbrake

Pilot's seat

Hand throttle

Pylon-strut strap

Passenger's seat

Main wing strut

Leading edge

Trailing edge

TRIKE UNIT

TWIN-CYLINDER ENGINE

Propeller-drive gearbox

Sealed lid

Twin carburetors

Air filter

Dual ignition plugs

Air-cooling fan

Exhaust connection

Engine rear mount

Metal hub

Waterproof stowage box

TRIKE NACELLE

EXHAUST PIPE

PROPELLER

WINGFRAME

Center-line beam

After muffler

Main exhaust muffler

Eyelet tensioning trailing edge to rib

Bracing cable

Rib

Single spar

King post

Leading edge

Semirigid fiberglass skin

Lift bracing wire

53

Navigation

ZERO READER (LANDING AID)

AERIAL NAVIGATION is the calculation of an aircraft's route from its point of departure to a given destination. It involves plotting the aircraft's course (heading) and airspeed, and the speed and direction of the wind (which will blow the aircraft off course). The resulting plotted line shows the track, or route, of the journey. Early pilots navigated using charts and visual aids such as landmarks; sometimes, they also used sextants to navigate by the stars. By 1920, cockpit radios could obtain a fix on an aircraft's position from ground stations or beacons. The introduction of radar in the 1940s made it possible to pinpoint the position of aircraft from the ground. Today, many small aircraft are still navigated using charts, radio, and simple hand-held instruments. Military aircraft and civil airliners are navigated using sophisticated on-board electronic systems, and signals from satellites that can be used to pinpoint an aircraft's position to within a few yards. The most advanced cockpits now display all navigational information on electronic screens.

DECCA TYPE 424 AIRFIELD RADAR, 1953

Parabolic reflector

Antenna mount

Tilt bearing

Main pedestal bearing

Weatherproof systems cabinet

Access door

NAVIGATOR'S CHART

Distance scales

Danger area

VHF omni-range (VOR) beacon

Ground station code and radio frequencies

Flight level of airway of 7,000 ft (2,130 m)

Airway name ("Amber 47")

Airway magnetic bearing of 239°

Compass rose centered on magnetic north

Airspace boundary

CIRCULAR SLIDE-RULE

Air-density correction window

True airspeed (TAS) scale

Minutes scale

Hours scale

Conversion scale between nautical miles and statute miles

Transparent cursor

Air-temperature window

Air-compressibility correction window

ELECTROMECHANICAL FLIGHT INSTRUMENTS

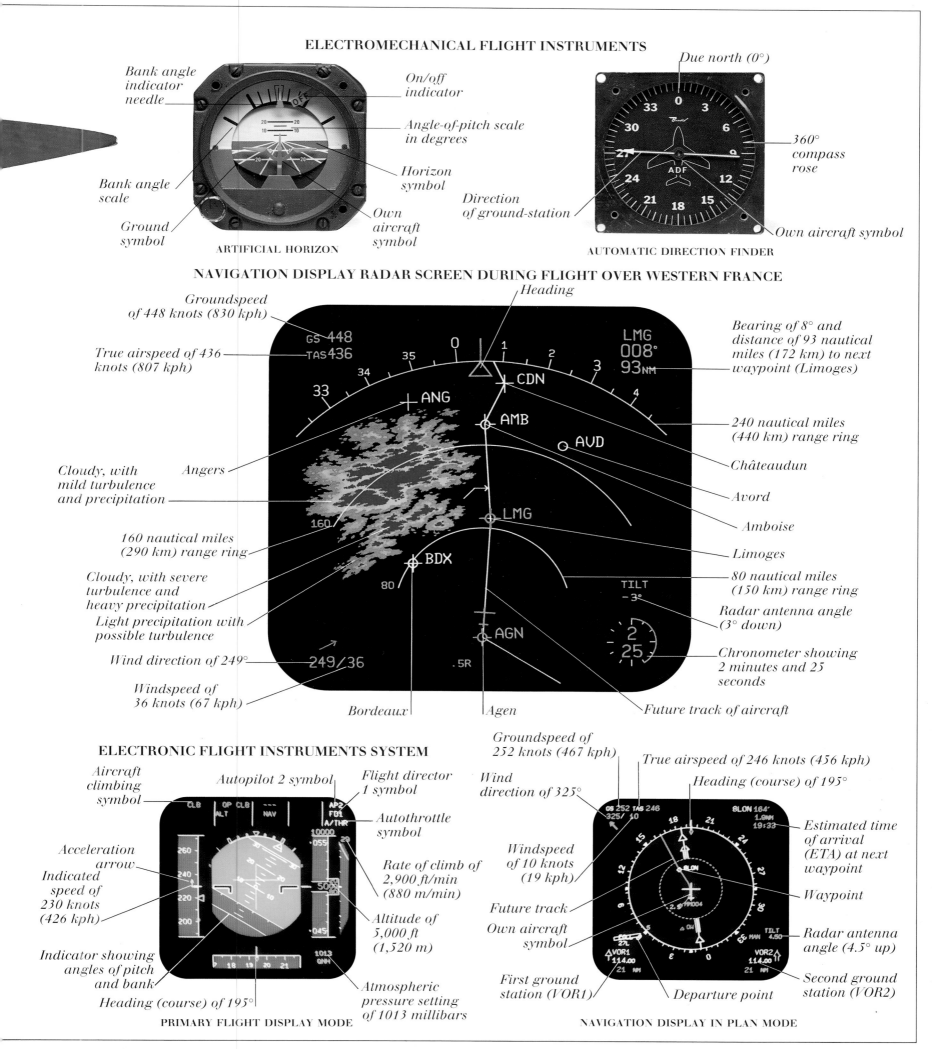

ARTIFICIAL HORIZON

Bank angle indicator needle
On/off indicator
Angle-of-pitch scale in degrees
Bank angle scale
Ground symbol
Horizon symbol
Own aircraft symbol

AUTOMATIC DIRECTION FINDER

Due north (0°)
360° compass rose
Direction of ground-station
Own aircraft symbol

NAVIGATION DISPLAY RADAR SCREEN DURING FLIGHT OVER WESTERN FRANCE

Groundspeed of 448 knots (830 kph)
True airspeed of 436 knots (807 kph)
Heading
Bearing of 8° and distance of 93 nautical miles (172 km) to next waypoint (Limoges)
240 nautical miles (440 km) range ring
Châteaudun
Avord
Amboise
Limoges
80 nautical miles (150 km) range ring
Radar antenna angle (3° down)
Chronometer showing 2 minutes and 25 seconds
Future track of aircraft
Agen
Bordeaux
Windspeed of 36 knots (67 kph)
Wind direction of 249°
Light precipitation with possible turbulence
Cloudy, with severe turbulence and heavy precipitation
160 nautical miles (290 km) range ring
Angers
Cloudy, with mild turbulence and precipitation

ELECTRONIC FLIGHT INSTRUMENTS SYSTEM

Aircraft climbing symbol
Autopilot 2 symbol
Flight director 1 symbol
Autothrottle symbol
Rate of climb of 2,900 ft/min (880 m/min)
Altitude of 5,000 ft (1,520 m)
Atmospheric pressure setting of 1013 millibars
Acceleration arrow
Indicated speed of 230 knots (426 kph)
Indicator showing angles of pitch and bank
Heading (course) of 195°

PRIMARY FLIGHT DISPLAY MODE

Groundspeed of 252 knots (467 kph)
True airspeed of 246 knots (456 kph)
Wind direction of 325°
Heading (course) of 195°
Estimated time of arrival (ETA) at next waypoint
Waypoint
Radar antenna angle (4.5° up)
Second ground station (VOR2)
Departure point
First ground station (VOR1)
Own aircraft symbol
Future track
Windspeed of 10 knots (19 kph)

NAVIGATION DISPLAY IN PLAN MODE

55

Safety and survival

FIRST AID KIT

S<small>INCE</small> W<small>ORLD</small> W<small>AR</small> I, <small>MOST AIRCRAFT</small> have carried various types of safety and survival equipment. Among the earliest survival items were fire extinguishers, parachutes, life jackets, and axes for breaking out of enclosed cabins. Today, airliners also carry oxygen masks that drop automatically from the cabin roof in emergencies; rapidly inflating rafts for use in emergency landings at sea; and inflatable escape slides to allow safe, fast descent from a grounded aircraft. Pilots of military aircraft wear pressurized suits equipped with an oxygen supply for high-altitude flight; the suits may also carry tools, rations, and weapons to aid survival in hostile environments. Combat aircraft have ejector seats that can shoot out of an aircraft at any height, even during supersonic flight. The seat's computer controls its flight and the deployment of the occupant's parachute. In addition to personal survival equipment, modern jetliners have various built-in safety features. Most mechanical parts are protected by smoke- and flame-detectors that trigger extinguishers if fire breaks out; as fuel is used, it is displaced in the tanks by non-inflammable inert gas; and every flight control system has a back-up system in case of mechanical or electrical failure. In addition, the most modern jetliners and military aircraft use computers to override commands from the pilot that could endanger the aircraft.

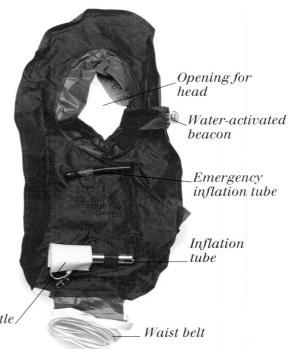

Opening for head

Water-activated beacon

Emergency inflation tube

Inflation tube

Air bottle

Waist belt

LIFE JACKET

PACKED LIFE JACKET

U.S. AIR FORCE SURVIVAL JACKET

Signal mirror

Compass

Hand-held signal flare

Tourniquet

Directional-strobe cover

Whistle

Nylon cord

Blanket

Battery

Battery-powered emergency strobe

First aid pack

Knife with sharpening stone

Nylon cord

Razor

Drinking-water container

Pistol holster

Survival vest

Utility knife

Ground-marker panels

Magnesium block with sparking insert for starting fires

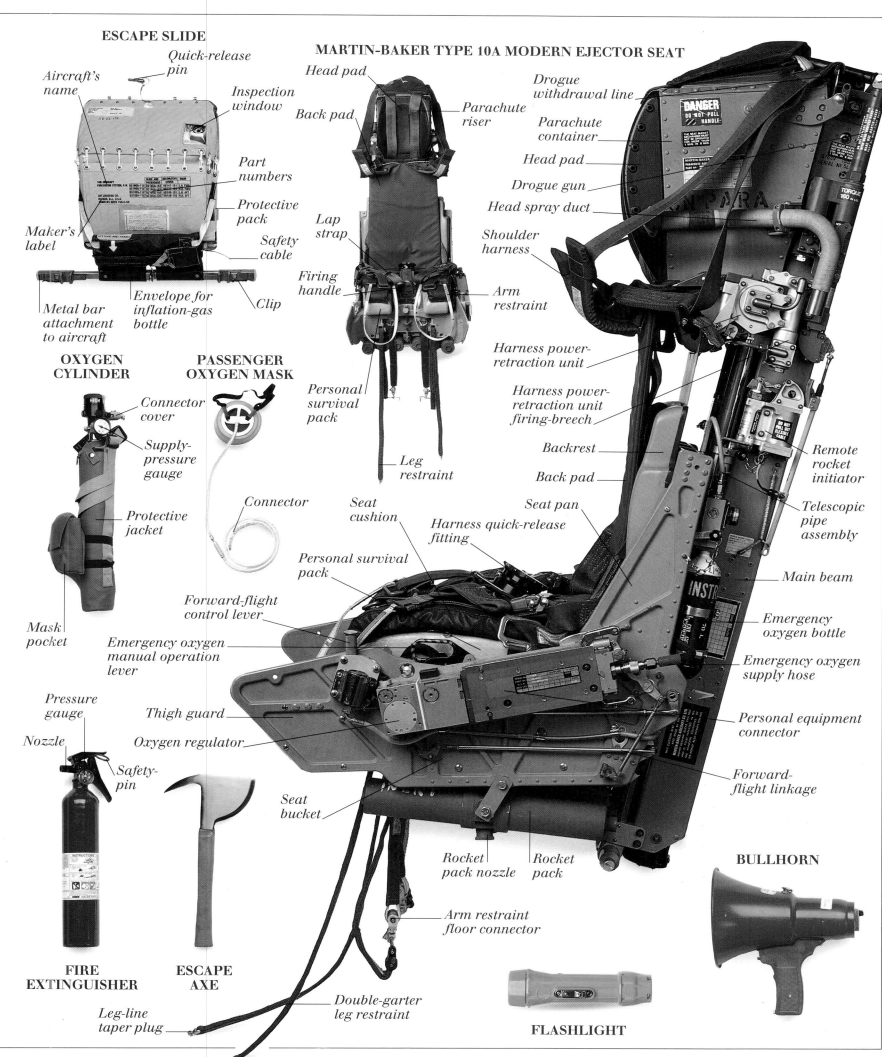

ESCAPE SLIDE

Quick-release pin

Aircraft's name

Inspection window

Part numbers

Protective pack

Safety cable

Maker's label

Metal bar attachment to aircraft

Envelope for inflation-gas bottle

Clip

MARTIN-BAKER TYPE 10A MODERN EJECTOR SEAT

Head pad

Back pad

Parachute riser

Drogue withdrawal line

Parachute container

Head pad

Drogue gun

Head spray duct

Shoulder harness

Lap strap

Firing handle

Arm restraint

Personal survival pack

Harness power-retraction unit

Harness power-retraction unit firing-breech

Leg restraint

Backrest

Back pad

Remote rocket initiator

Telescopic pipe assembly

Main beam

Emergency oxygen bottle

Emergency oxygen supply hose

Personal equipment connector

Forward-flight linkage

OXYGEN CYLINDER

Connector cover

Supply-pressure gauge

Protective jacket

Mask pocket

PASSENGER OXYGEN MASK

Connector

Seat cushion

Seat pan

Harness quick-release fitting

Personal survival pack

Forward-flight control lever

Emergency oxygen manual operation lever

Thigh guard

Oxygen regulator

Seat bucket

Rocket pack nozzle

Rocket pack

Arm restraint floor connector

Pressure gauge

Nozzle

Safety-pin

FIRE EXTINGUISHER

ESCAPE AXE

Leg-line taper plug

Double-garter leg restraint

BULLHORN

FLASHLIGHT

57

VTOL aircraft

THE FIRST VTOL (VERTICAL TAKEOFF AND LANDING) aircraft were helicopters. For fixed-wing aircraft, VTOL became a realistic possibility when the British aircraft engine manufacturer Rolls-Royce pioneered the "Flying Bedstead" in 1953. This device consisted of simply a wingless four-legged frame with two jet engines pointing downward. It made the first ever vertical takeoff using jet-power, and eventually led to the development of the British Hawker Siddeley Harrier (later built by British Aerospace). The Harrier was the first VTOL airplane with sufficient power and maneuverability to carry out the duties for which it was designed. Its single engine is a Rolls-Royce Pegasus turbofan with four nozzles. All four nozzles are vectored (rotated) downward for VTOL or hovering, and rearward for high-speed flight. In the USA, a different type of VTOL airplane has been pioneered using special tilting rotors. This aircraft—the Bell-Boeing V-22 Osprey—has a jet-turbine-powered "proprotor" on each wingtip. For vertical takeoff, hovering, and landing, the proprotors are tilted upward and act as helicopter rotors; for normal flight, the proprotors are gradually tilted forward to act as conventional propellers.

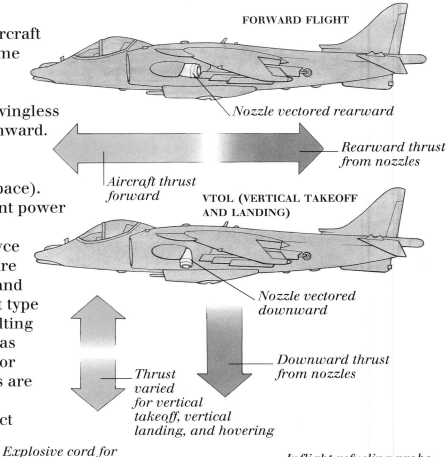

FORWARD FLIGHT

Nozzle vectored rearward

Aircraft thrust forward

Rearward thrust from nozzles

VTOL (VERTICAL TAKEOFF AND LANDING)

Nozzle vectored downward

Downward thrust from nozzles

Thrust varied for vertical takeoff, vertical landing, and hovering

SIDE VIEW OF HARRIER GR5

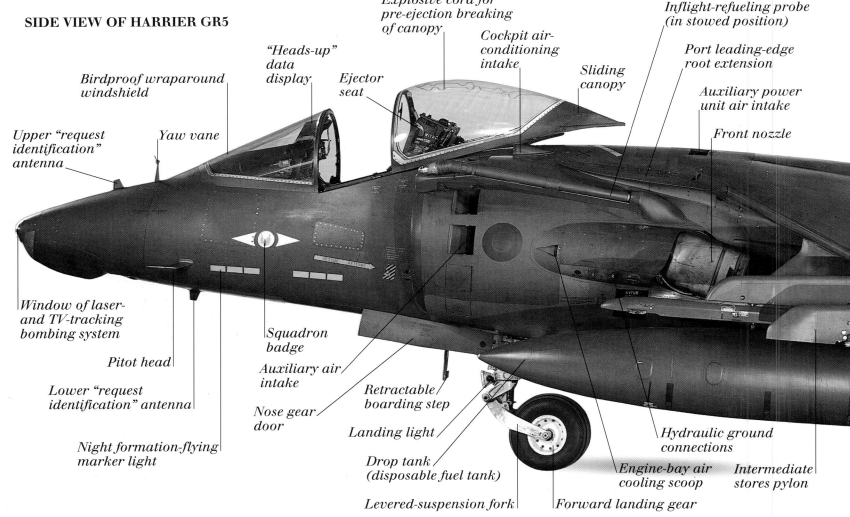

Explosive cord for pre-ejection breaking of canopy

Inflight-refueling probe (in stowed position)

Cockpit air-conditioning intake

"Heads-up" data display

Ejector seat

Sliding canopy

Port leading-edge root extension

Birdproof wraparound windshield

Auxiliary power unit air intake

Yaw vane

Front nozzle

Upper "request identification" antenna

Window of laser- and TV-tracking bombing system

Squadron badge

Pitot head

Auxiliary air intake

Retractable boarding step

Hydraulic ground connections

Lower "request identification" antenna

Nose gear door

Landing light

Night formation-flying marker light

Drop tank (disposable fuel tank)

Engine-bay air cooling scoop

Intermediate stores pylon

Levered-suspension fork

Forward landing gear

FRONT VIEW OF HARRIER GR5

Sliding canopy

Rearview mirror

Birdproof wraparound windshield

Yaw vane

Engine air-intake-duct inner wall

Upper "request identification" antenna

Engine air intake lip

Inflight-refueling probe

Fuel tank pylon

Aerodynamic fence

Anhedral (downward-sloping) wing

Row of vortex generators

Passive radar warning antenna

Outboard stores pylon

Sidewinder air-to-air missile launcher

Front nozzle

Port air intake

Intermediate stores pylon

Drop tank (disposable fuel tank)

Starboard gun pod

Window of laser- and TV-tracking bombing system

Outrigger landing gear

Retractable boarding step

Twin-wheel main landing gear

Lift-improvement fence

Landing light

Hydraulically steered nose gear

VHF blade antenna

Communications antenna fairing

Anti-collision strobe light

Night formation-flying marker light

Row of vortex generators

Low-band radar warning antenna

Radar warning antenna looking forward

Outrigger wheel fairing

Fin

Rudder

Roll-control reaction jet

Heat exchanger air intake (ram scoop)

Yaw-control reaction jet

Flap

Aileron

Air vent

Radome

ZD408

Tail plane

Formation light strip

Port navigation light

Night formation-flying marker light

Outrigger door

Aircraft serial number

Ventral fin

Tail bumper

Rearward-jamming transmitter antenna

Main landing gear

Outrigger landing gear

Broad-band communications antenna

Radar warning antenna looking rearward

Low-band radar warning antenna

59

Index

63

Acknowledgments

Dorling Kindersley would like to thank the following:

Aeromega Helicopters, Stapleford, for the Bell Jetranger; Aero Shopping, London, for instruments (p. 54); Avionics Mobile Services Ltd, Watford, for instruments (p. 55); Roy Barber and John Chapman, RAF Museum, Hendon, for the BE 2B, flying helmet, Gnome cylinder, Hawker Hart trainer, Hawker Tempest, le Rhône engine, and Rolls-Royce Kestrel engine; Mitch Barnes Aviation, London, for instruments (pp. 16-17); Mike Beach for the Curtiss-D Pusher; British Caledonian Flight Training Ltd for the Airbus flight deck simulator; Fred Coates, Helitech (Luton) Ltd, for the Bell-47 components; Michael Cuttell and CSE Aviation Ltd, Oxford, for the Bell-47 and Schweizer 300; Dowty Aerospace Landing Gear, Gloucester; Guy Hartcup of the Airship Association for advice; Anthony Hooley, Chris Walsh, and David Cord, British Aerospace Regional Aircraft Ltd, for the BAe-146 jetliner, safety equipment, and computer-designed SST; Ken Huntley, Mid-West Aero Engines Ltd, for engines (pp. 26-27); Imperial War Museum, Duxford, for Concorde; The London Gliding Club, Dunstable, for the Schleicher K23; Musée des Ballons, Calvados, for the statoscope; Noel Penny Turbines Ltd for the turbojet; Andy Pavey, Aviation Scotland Ltd, for the ARV Super 2; Tony Pavey, Thermal Aircraft Developments, London, for the gas cylinder, balloon basket and burner, and navigator's chart; the Commanding Officer and personnel of RAF St. Athan for the Tornado and ejector seat; the Commanding Officer and personnel of RAF Wittering for the Harrier; The Science Museum, London, for the Montgolfier balloon, Schütte-Lanz airship, Armstrong Siddeley engine, instruments (p. 16), and propeller (p. 12); Ross Sharp, The Science Museum, Wroughton, for the Lockheed Electra, airfield radar, Handley Page Gugnunc, and magneto; The Shuttleworth Collection for the Avro Lynx cockpit panel, Avro Triplane IV, Avro Tutor, Blackburn monoplane, Blériot XI, Bristol cockpit,

LVG CVI, and Wright Flyer; Skysport Engineering for the Bristol fighter wing; Mike Smith for the survival jacket; Solar Wings Ltd, Marlborough, for the Pegasus Quasar ultralight; Julian Temple, Brooklands Museum Trust Ltd, for the Vickers Viking, Vickers Wellington, and Curtiss-D Pusher; Kelvin Wilson, Flying Start, for the Pegasus XL SE ultralight

Special thanks to David Learmount for invaluable editorial advice

Additional design assistance:

Alexandra Brown, Paul Calver, Clare Shedden, Bryn Walls, Ellen Woodward

Additional editorial assistance:

Nicholas Jackson, Paul Jackson, Mary Lindsay, Bob Ogden, Louise Tucker

Additional illustration:

Simone End

Additional photography:

Peter Chadwick, Andy Crawford, Mike Dunning, David Exton, Gary Kevin, Dave King, Dave Rudkin

Picture credits:

p. 19 top left, p. 52 top left: Austin Brown and the Aviation Picture Library; p. 40 top left: British Aerospace (Commercial Aircraft) Ltd; pp. 42-43 bottom, p. 43 top: Pratt & Whitney Canada; p. 55 centre: the Quadrant Picture Library